A KITE'S DINNER

SHEILA WINGFIELD

A KITE'S DINNER

POEMS 1938–1954

*The heart is a small thing,
but desireth great matters.
It is not sufficient for a
kite's dinner, yet the whole
world is not sufficient for it.*

ANON. 12TH CENT.

THE CRESSET PRESS

1954

First published in 1954 by
The Cresset Press Ltd.
11 Fitzroy Square, London, W.1
and printed in Great Britain by
The Shenval Press Ltd., London, Hertford and Harlow

AUTHOR'S NOTE

This collection is made up of the only poems I wish kept from my previously published work. A number of revisions have been made.

None of the verse in the last section has appeared in book form before.

I wish to thank the Editors of *The Dublin Magazine*, *The Times Literary Supplement*, *The New Statesman & Nation*, and *The London Magazine* for permission to reprint certain poems.

CONTENTS

FROM 'POEMS' (1938)

'BEAT DRUM, BEAT HEART' (1946)

vii

From 'Poems' (1938)

ODYSSEUS DYING

I think Odysseus, as he dies, forgets
Which was Calypso, which Penelope,
Only remembering the wind that sets
Off Mimas, and how endlessly
His eyes were stung with brine;
Argos a puppy, leaping happily;
And his old Father digging round a vine.

WINTER

The tree still bends over the lake,
And I try to recall our love,
Our love which had a thousand leaves.

A BIRD

Unexplained
In the salt meadow
Lay the dead bird.
The wind
Was fluttering its wings.

3

EPITAPH

The heart that leapt
To hear shots ringing through a winter wood
Or feel a boat heel, trembling, to the sea;
That at the tale of the dog Argos wept
And loved the summer thickness of a tree:
Shame that it should
Be stilled into eternity.

A WOMAN

You laugh as did the dancing tide
That lifted Venus from the waves.
What treasure lies
Upon the sea-floor of your eyes?
And do you hide
Your sighing in rock caves?

TRIPTYCH

From mulberry air which feels
Folded in thickness,
Her dress where she passes
Catching in spiked grasses
And glaucous aloe,

Her child and she, breathless,
Towards Egypt go.

Bleached are all noises
And brittle the mornings;
Chip of builders who cling
To golden scaffolding,
And shouts, will not drown
These tinklings and brayings
In Hierusalemes town.

Such greyness of misery
None else knows.
Three men crouch, asleep;
Still as a stone they keep:
The world in its plight
Cannot halt a cockcrow's
Curl in paling night.

THE CHIEFTAIN

And when he took his grief
Into the gentle-breasted hills,
He felt clouds marching, and the wind
Unheeded and unheeding pass
Through smallest bilberries in leaf
And the tough mountain grass,

Until he could no longer bear
The pressing of his soul,
And prayed to be released from self, from name,
To mingle senseless with the air
Some little time. But as within his mind
The oar would not desert its thole,
To his dark courtyard back he came
Uncomforted of all his ills.

CHOSROE THE SECOND

You who are happy to attend
   The gorgeous rotting of the year,
   Gather your robes and hear
   How Chosroe, king of Persia, nears his end.

In bedstuffs of brocade he lies
   Unmoving, while his shadowed eyes
   Can only stare
   Into the dark, because a screaming jay
   Of thought flashed from his son's head
   To take the throne as prey,
   Confine him in the palace, and there
   Starve him dead.

'The people smiled upon my son:
   I feared; I held his flutter in a cage;

6

But they rose up and freed him, and his rage
Now makes me carrion.
Oh, for the wind,
The bronze bits and the spume,
And earthy pebbles flying from our way;
Or could I from the windowsill
One moment lean,
To snuff looseness of air that lies between
Orion and the medlar's bloom;
Or cease to mind
That, carved in the bed's ornament,
These little squirrels still will play
Among their grapes when I am spent.'

So Chosroe grieves, until
For Caryatides he begs,
With lifted arms and fluted legs,
To bear his sorrow through the night
On marble napes with all their might;
For now, out of his pillared groves have flown
The twittering councillors, and all
Is quiet as a forest, where alone
Slow-dropping fruits of hour or minute fall.

'It was a princely morning of bright winds
When flags, the horses of the air, were prancing mad,
That I inherited
The kingdom, glad

To send my armies striding like the sun,
Their cheeks now warmed by summer's grass
Of unknown kinds,
Now chilled by mountain pass,
Until to Antioch and Damascus they had run;
And leaving quays behind them bleached
Like bones, and streets dry as a riverbed,
Three times Chalcedon reached;
Then on to lands,
For bases, among winds and sands
And creaking phoenix palms, where sing
Cicadas noisy as the surf; as well
As watching on the Hellespont, whose boats
Can in their westering
Touch the salt-bitten leaves, and seaweed floats
Up-river on the swell.
My embassies have been
Where little horsemen, for a moment seen,
Are swirled in mountain mist;
While here, as on a list
Of tumbled cities, I can spell
Jerusalem, whose shuffling crowds
I massacred to stain her floors
And take her Cross of the acacia tree;
Palmyra, empty save for a garrison
Who whistle in the open doors;
And many others that have winged me on
To the far hills or mirrored clouds.

' "Sire, I find the skies in doubt
   And statues weeping."
   Now our lances in the field
   Rattled as leaves October winds have dried;
   Now hawks and patridges that wheeled
   Above the dancing blades could tell
   Our columns—usually a stream
   That in its flow only a moment parts
   For hostile, elbowing rocks—
   Were trickles, creeping,
   And then drained without a gleam;
   Now loudly as the shingle knocks
   Beneath a drawn-up wave, our clashing pride
   Was overwhelmed; and when, at Nineveh,
   My troops that had set out
   All scaled in armour like a morning sea,
   By dusk lay on the plain with smoking hearts,
   I knew my kingdom fallen like a tree.

'Back into the earth's caul
   I soon must go,
   Leaving this useless air
   To some old villager
   Who sits against his cottage wall
   And plantlike feels the wind and sun.
   You gods of light and darkness, blow,
   Blow on my little spark, so nearly done.'

Then Chosroe puts his cooling lips
   Upon the black flute of the night, to dream
   That his own breath
   Becomes a tune that coiling, drifts,
   Unable to retain its theme,
   Until in gentle rifts
   Each moment thinner blown, it slips
   At last into the endless space of death.

ADVICE

   I ask: Can you no longer find
   Doors to the township of her mind?
   And are her thoughts, that like a cloud
   Of starlings wheeled with yours, too proud
   And single in their flight? You nod. So
   Cease your wooing: you should know
   Warm Daphne cannot be remade
   Out of the dark laurel shade.
   Leave her; to wild islands go
   Or green-domed cities caped in snow;
   To roughened lakes whose yellow froth
   Is bitter as a god's wrath;
   Where nymphs, afraid of being burned
   By love, have into rivers turned;
   Or where through mountain gorges spurred
   That prince behind a golden bird;
   Ride on the horny backs of seas

10

To meet bright-cottoned ebonies:
Wander, uneasy as the tides,
Until your renegade decides—
Watching the chimney-cowls all bare
And silent in the snowy air,
Her forehead numbed by window-pane—
She needs to feel your heart again.

THE DEAD

The wind that blew the plumes astray
And bore the trumpet noise away
Has so effaced the dead
And thinned them to so fine a mist
That, harried in a drove
Of fellow ghosts, they run ahead
Beyond our reach. This wind, from barrack square
Or from the asphalt near some tenement,
Does it persist
In hinting that immortals should prepare
To shiver in a leafless grove?—
A jealous wind, that will steal half
Of the hot meadow's reaper-clack
Which is all summer, or the night-stock's scent,
Or, on the road, a friend's laugh,
And pleases to hurl back
Smoke or broken tiles where urchins shout;

That makes the sobbing wavelets curl,
While neither reed nor rush escapes
The impress of its hurrying seal;
Giving our tongue a pennant's furl,
Turning a sleeper's thoughts to untrue shapes;
A stubborn wind, that thickens till you feel
A door bang: and then memory's shut out.

The quiet dead,
Who were decoyed by a false tale
Of murmurings on Lethe's pebbly bed,
Have cast from them as childishness our joy
In live and woken things which yet, may now
Be part of their own foolish, constant dreams,
And are aloof from how
We long to peer behind the murk
And pantomime of bony jowl
And yew and headstone, to unveil
Their voices or their children's screams,
Or how they hummed and paused at work.
But tautly as you dare to strain
In listening, you only hear again
Hector to Aias calling like an owl,
At night, across the wasted plain of Troy.

In spite of this we strive
With vigour, when alive,
For earthen perpetuity;

In spite of the small bones that lie
In hills, green-lidded from the light;
In spite of that Imperial road
Where warriors stand in their huge stone
And wildflowers blow about their feet; in spite
Of nothing being colder than the rain
On knees of monuments, or mute as fame
From trumpets with the angel gilt;
Though manifold can be a name
As is the wind's print on the seas
And yet will fade in libraries,
Or few as those in thymy air
Found carved on a Pentelic chair;
Though this one is as neat
As a lark's shadow, that one grown
To a forbidding, dark domain;
Though we as children left the teat
And then, full grown, from folly strode:
Yet do we want our tower built,
Or great Sikander's marching cloud of dust,
Each breath, each step, with aching thrust.

RESOLVE

From his high room which looks on woods and plain
Telemachus leans out and dreams again
Of searching for his Father, while the Nurse

Now folds his clothes, now puts away his purse,
Now sets the sheepskin on the bed: until
The day he goes with brisk and certain will.
No longer, Muse, no longer shall I wait
To seek what I hold loved and rare and great.

A WOMAN BY HER HEARTH

By the sea-swell that once Arabia wore,
By goats that brought a desert evermore
To where much tamarisk and cassia grew,
By rosy Helen, bright-eyed like a bird,
Who from her turrets with young Paris flew
Before so many homes by war were seared,
And by the sadness of the hound beside
The lake where lover-wounded Procris died,

I take my honest oath that I prefer
The drip from twigs under a steady rain
To being centred in wild hurricane,
Hedges to moors, a village street to quays,
The many-fingered ash to mango's trees,
A rushy meadow to such crags as kill,
And hearing carts that crackle up a hill
To sheering in the winds, a traveller:

For here, returned to the kind fields and grange
And comfortable woods which never change,

Away from that disordered sea of love
Storm haunted and most traitorous with grief,
I can as clearly as a bird-call prove
How life, slow-branching into quiet leaf,
Fills with content the turning of my years
As each true season's ritual appears.

A LOVER SPEAKS OF HIS CONTRADICTION

I know a summer morning when the rivermist
Will hang like Beauty's breath upon her glass;
Yet among streets where crowds pass,
In living I persist,
And cry 'Alas'.

Remembering the gentler waters, I regret
Their hush on a far, sleeping shore at night;
Yet choose for pleasure a chill fight
With tides, and the stiff net,
And rain's bite.

When gods were calling from the trees like birds, we
    were
At ease in our beliefs, while now the mind
Has come to open land whose wind
Lays bare; yet I prefer
It thus unkind.

I want above all mortal things to hold my dove
And feel the murmur in her throat. You
Are but dark flight, the flash and sinew
And the fierce eye of love;
Yet I pursue.

YOUNG ARGONAUTS

In a small bitterness of wind
The reeds divided, as we felt
Our keel slide over stones, and smelt

The lough all round us. Soon the trace
Of shore was further than the sight
Of wildbirds crying in their flight;

But now the waves are paler finned,
The water blacker, we are blown
To somewhere strange and yet foreknown:

This is the Euxine, this the place—
Row on, row on, to catch the gold
In dripping fleece, as they of old.

THE JOURNEY

1

Pale as his February twigs,
The ditcher, as he cuts and digs,
Thinks of his hearth. But I, alone
And cold as iron, would disown
A countryside whose lack and stint
Empty the mind—where seldom, flint
Strikes a boot-tip into spark;
Where rolling mists erase each mark;
And pollards in a flooded field
Can see their neediness revealed.
As foxes are impelled yet loath
To leave the dripping undergrowth
That frets their nerves all day, so Spring
Drives me to restive wandering.

2

I will set out to journey through
Flat lands and the slow forest; you,
In crossing the warm straits, will pass
Such clouds as in their moonlit glass
Must dream of swans; by several
Opposing roads at last we shall—
In park or theatre or the street—
Be startled, yet prepared, to meet.
Then will our joy be to divide

The spoils we see on every side,
And as we travel on, to swear
By the whole might of sunset, where
The tightly wooded hills roll down
Into the shadow of its frown,
To trust in it where it repays
A river with a gilded haze,
Or at the mountain's edge invoke
Its roaring fire and plains that smoke;
To come to a great lake, and vow
In silence, where the moon is now
A loose-scaled serpent that must dance
On formless water's blackest glance.
Leaving the towns of jostled cries,
Where men have languor and quick eyes,
We wake to bells and to the chirp
Of unknown birds, and then usurp
A noonday glaring of white stone
That blinded Caesars, by our own
Dazzle of laughter; we acclaim
Ferocities of rock now tame
And husbanded where earth and terrace,
Brown as an old gardener's face,
Wrinkle at dusk; we hear the slight
Tumble of fruit that measures night.
Onward again, more slowly, each
Warmed by a harvest plain, to reach
The empty mirrors, footless floors,

Where water fondles marble doors,
And in the darkness of an arch
A figure stands, and throngs will march
On bridges with a silent tread.
But here our pattern must unthread
Its ended line, for suddenly
You leave me searching hopelessly.
The awning moves without a sound
In heaviness of air around
My head, as leaning from my window,
Chin in hands, I let a slow,
An undefended sadness fill
The evening and the night, until
The dawn wind, shivering the trees
By the still shuttered houses, sees
My heart to be a swollen tide
Whose flood I can no longer ride.

3

Back from a whirling of white dust
To where the beeches shed their rust
Under the loaded, rain-dark clouds,
I note—away from talk or crowds—
A haystack's clearly shadowed cut,
The turned earth, and a friendly rut;
I grasp a stick of well-known notch
And smoothness in my palm; I watch,
Where winter oaks have always stood,

A pheasant slide into a wood;
I mark the hushed, the bleak appeal
Of the long pastureland, and feel
The snow-sky like a pigeon's breast
Hold me entranced and repossessed.

A FRIEND

As Constantine could proudly pace
The outline of his marble town
On hummocks and on open down,

So, when I met you, did I trace
What cupolas and columns rare
Might rise into a morning air,

What boats might glide and bridges span,
What streets unwind for us to walk
In crowds and dusk and endless talk;

But never, never did I plan
These cracked walls by a tumbled door,
Deserted even by the poor.

THE HOURS

1

The hill lifts off her mist, as slow
As goddesses unrobe their feet,
And over spires and rooftops cling
The flushed veils of the morning's heat;
But gradually, to and fro,
We hear a pulsing in the street,
Rattle of window and of wheel,
Or cries, or river freshening:
Brisk and seaward in their flow,
The urgent ripples make us feel
A need to hammer through the world,
Or sail to where small islands lift,
To ride beside the wind, or shift
Great rocks that once the giants hurled.

2

Noon with his compass legs will walk
Across meridians of the sea,
And for a while, watch with the hawk
A salty shrub in Tartary,
The council of the mountain crests,
A tortoise quivering a stalk
Of barley, or a man that rests
Under a Syrian almond tree;
And when the sun's unbarriered track

Reaches the downs, and from his groove
He slants his heat upon my back,
I pry through trellis of the vetch
And spotted cloverleaf, and move
A forest with a fingerstretch.

3

Look from your windows, lovers, lean
On bridges in the warm, tired air,
For now is evening poised between
Light-hearted day and the dark's snare,
Like a girl flirting in her glass
And softly letting down her hair.
The little moths in seeding grass
Flutter their life out through the field
Where starwort gleams, and as you pass,
All colours that have loudly made
A dying declaration, yield
In whispers to the very shade
Of lichen, and of sheep that browse
Dimly below orchard boughs.

4

Alone among night-scented leaves
Must Sargon's daughter, pining, tend
Her charge, the Babylonian moon;
While others, like the leaning sheaves
That now in darkness seem to blend,

Make love; it is the hour when soon
St. Jerome, putting down his quill,
Unlatches to the secret friend,
Then works, with all Judaea still;
When some will wake at horror's edge,
And women start the pains of birth;
When careful paws creep out to kill
And a bird twitches in the hedge,
While dreams smoke from the quiet Earth

VINCENT SQUARE

Come, Autumn, blow the sounds about
Of footsteps and of leaves,
For it is time we did without
The languor that deceives
Events with wishes, facts with doubt,
In the long summer eves;
Come, bring your blustering to rout
What softens or aggrieves.

Let a lad's whistle, scream of train,
Be carried on a gust
Of thought which snatches up the skein
Of what is firm and just;
Let pavements hiss in the night rain,
And tugboats hoot and thrust
Into our sleep, till we regain
Those dreams, for dream we must.

THE WILL

Determined to outlive
Old Death, I here dispose
Of my own self, to give
In equal shares to those

Who catch their breath and run
Where kites fly on a common
As they tug the string,
And in a boistering
Of clouds can see these chase
Far steeples in a race,
And hear how larks will bridge
The airs on chalky ridge;

To those who, in the night,
Press with a mob's delight
Between close laughter,
Music over water,
And such rockets as are
Greener than the Dogstar
In the pitchy sky
And then as Venus rosy;

And to all those beside
Some mooring where the tide
Slaps against a wall
In tireless rise and fall;

Who know the seas off Ushant,
And the double chant
Of Goodwins, North and South,
And the dark rivermouth;

Who, with a quickened heart,
Watch heavy curtains part
And, as the scene is acted,
From a turn of head
Will hear the distant fair,
Or smell a citroned air,
Or feel crowds in the rain
Crying in boundless pain;

To one as, working, looks
At the burnt-paper rooks
Blown by a gale, or rare
Wild swans, or at a fieldfare
Twirking from a copse,
Or over the trees' tops
Excited pigeons, high
And swerving with quick eye;

To anyone who likes
To stand near seething dykes
Or millwheels' churning foam,
Or branches as they comb
The fierce back of a spate,
Or the neat weirs, or great

Down-curling plumes that fall
Into tremendous brawl;

Whose friends in talking stay
Wise, proud or gay,
And curve their lip, and frown
And shut their eyelids down,
Disputing, and then smile
In fond and gentle guile,
Their face grooved, and their mind
Unfettered as the wind;

And such as love the fret
Where streets lisp in the wet
And starling thousands twitter
In a London square;
Where men, so torn and tried
From Barnet to Bankside,
Most splendidly provoke
The sunset's angered smoke.

I think they smile who know—
Signing a Testament—
That all they now bestow
Will prove to have been spent.

SONNET

Jordan that feeds from far Mount Hermon's snow,
Thames with its fogs and warehouses and docks,
Dargle whose alders dip on little rocks,
The Nile where heavily feluccas go,
Untroubled Avon in flat watermeadow
Or the mad pacing Rhine of many shocks,
Medway that swings the tackle through the blocks,
Deben now still, but for two boys who row;
The waters that will storm a city's gate
Or lie in glazing pools above a slope,
Or lessen, or become immoderate:
All these I feel within me and their scope
Carried by veins throughout my whole estate,
So quiet is my face and wild my hope.

'*Beat Drum, Beat Heart*' (1946)

PART ONE

MEN IN WAR

Shouts rang up the street
War War it has come
Like leaves they were blown:
A spear from its corner
A summons on paper
Or buckle to thumb:

In the dark of a room
Old fears were known
By wrinkled up cheeks
And by young wives
Bent back at the waist
To kiss them alone:

But light were their feet
As thoughts were broken
And barriers thrown—
Out of copse out of brake
Out of field they were flown
To the tap of the drum.

✻

Goodbye the milkcart pony
Standing in the sun;
The creaking basket
Of a baker's round;
And summer's garden besom
Sweeping on the ground
Then pausing; work unfinished
And work done.

Goodbye to the inn's warmth
Of views on beer and crop,
Where each man's talk
Is well known as his gait;
Goodbye to what the village
Knows and hears; to that late
Word at the lit door
Of a small shop.

Goodbye such emptiness
As loiters up and down
To show its friends
The new pup on a string,
Or with some tight-held flowers
Goes mutely visiting,
On Sundays, in the cleanness
Of a town.

✻

All this is gone, a lost age,
Gust-torn like a picture page
That flutters, sidles down, then lies:
For a new sight now stings men's eyes
As, carried in a wind that sweeps
Them over shores and crags,—what steeps
They'll view, how take a city's height,
Where their force will next alight
Or like a spark will strike the sea,
Into what gates they bring a key—
Not one among the many knows.
But hopefully a trumpet echoes
Under arch of colonnade;
And shivering but unafraid
Others in pale air will roll
With bedding and with bamboo pole,
Plank cart and piebald pony,
Jerking over hills and *li*.
Look at them, at march or rest:
A gipsy walking gave the breast
To this one, and he likes to feel
Peril snapping at his heel;
While him, that Dublin bucko there,
At Liffey's edge who'd spit and swear,
Now whistles 'Killaloe' quite plain
Through the drenching Flemish rain;
Another, that in passing smiles
With pleasure at the red-curled tiles

Of homes; or he whose limbs are free,
Or knobbed like Kentish cobnut tree;
Pale Yorkshireman with eager gullet
And lank wrist—each one is yet
That god the Mexicans have sung
Who was in Paradise made young.
You will have heard some call them mad.
But whether any of them had
A doubt, which for a moment stood
Shy as roebuck in a wood
Before it fled in shadowed haste,
Is forgotten and effaced;
Or whether, to the night air
Extending patiently and where
Lyra throbs and Lynx spies
And Draco's coils anatomize,
They turned for help, with dry lips,
Pumping heart, wet fingertips
And gulping breath   historian
Or plaque will never say.   All I can
Tell is, that as clouds which seem
Too soft may harden till they gleam
Like iron shields, then clash their scorn
Downward, by veined anger torn;
As fire through Leinster's bowels ranged;
Or as the French king's blood was changed
Who saw the Englishmen at Cressy;
As a pibroch's wail would free

Some heavy sword from off its strap
And give the plaid a tighter wrap;
    As on a gentle morning, youths
    To whom a lute, a rose, were truths,
Fought from thick-rigged galleass
With savagery that saved the Mass;
    As those by nature wise and mild,
    Twelve provinces of forest and wild
Rivers, terrors, ravines crossed
And mountains, half their number lost,
    On the Long March which lasted three days
    And a year: so war will braze
My metal. I declare, that with the oldest
Of our ills pressed on me, borne on me like
    A storm which no mere plan can shift
    Or strength dispel, with danger turned
From a low thunder rolling in the hills
To an immediate hurt, I am aware
    No time but now ever existed,
    This was I meant for, here I am man:
Which—before a fox saw villages
Die out when the Euphrates changed its bed,
    Or lazy air first woke to tower,
    Or hunters could hear northern winds,
While grasses whipped their legs, moan in the rocks—
Men learned, men knew, men felt, men understood.
    The fact is proved and clear, that war
    Rescinds what mattered, rends each form.

My hand, no longer casual and loose plucking
Under a filtering of trellised leaves,
 With careful and slight trigger act
 Gives vast effect; wishes once scattered,
Vague as any drift of gipsies, have now
Gathered from their road and ditch and plain
 Into one march of power; thoughts that were
 Finches starting from a thicket
Wing to where the eagle and the sun
Beat fiercely in a far and dazzled reach,
 High from the ground's indignity:
 Witness how David, rid of foes,
Grieves most; and Caesar sets up Pompey's statue;
Over Alps how emperors can boast
 In fight and Holy, then, be crowned.
 O praise events that led me to this
Fate, whose searchlight-cone, or glint on hilt
Points out the place where I can show my whole
 And candid self: let me be great,
 Bold, gilt by that esteem
Each lover longs for in a woman's eyes
To flood his soul with bliss and to uphold
 Supreme compulsion and desire
 With governance, salvation, succour,
Monstrous commands, and favour.   Let me die:
Cut out my heart and hold it to the sun
 In fury; may its blood run slowly
 Under root and stone of time,

To rise in temples where ash-whitened Shiva,
The abhorred, renews by fire, and urge
   Crusaders in far massacre
   To tread the winepress of the Lord.

Brothers, this is our cloud, our hidden night.
We, being obscured ourselves, know nothing,
   In this darkness find no frame,
   No ladder to climb in clear air,
No tap or chip of bricks on a bright day;
But lean together as if chained to pillars,
   Under scourge from the whole world.
   And now not I, but at all cost
The other, must be saved from harm. Look how
In chaos they are carrying a boy
   On strong arms, with safe steps, or lifting
   In the half-drowned enemy,
Their names lost like a voice in the storm, shown
On the scroll of the sea, hushed in passages
   And space of air, of empty windy
   Air, or shouted by a noise
Uncurling to implacable explosion,
Then vanished, gone. Note how in this turmoil
   It is strange as myth to meet
   A man who sows his land in calm,
A pigeon nest, joy of a watermill:
For in our blood we feel the heavy pace
   Of cataracts and, in our limbs,

The tremor of small leaves that shake
Beside them, on their banks, perpetually.
We are a madness, shrill over the ground,
　　We are the bass notes' melancholy;
　　We are the men who pulled Lorca
Between arches by tall-shadowed houses;
We are a man dragged and killed on the outskirts
　　Of a town in Spain. We know both
　　Chill and warmth of the guerillas
Lumbering through snow, defending Moscow;
The shelterwarden's knack of seeming mild,
　　His inner rage. Another time,
　　Close under the soil we go
In trenches, huddled in a reek of furs,
Like pictures in a bestiary: for cunning,
　　Fellowship and cruelty
　　Live in my palms and shins and back;
And glitter-eyed, like flocks at night, are those
Who camp in dips and hollows of a field.
　　Each thing that stirs, warily
　　Is watched and feared and felt and spied,
And silence, or the din of gunfire, guessed
For signs. Sappers have kneeled; they tap and wait
　　And listen for the faint of sounds,
　　Then know their fate. O smile O cry
For minutes hang on rumours of a rumour,
Hours fall to a wreck, and seconds beat
　　As in Cassandra's pulsing neck

With my defeat or with your doom,
With answer to our two encountered ranks,
With hurts, much longing, sickness and huge dread.
   To bear it is the test of war
   Or love: the plume of bravery.

But look, how this one's glad and how he grips
His steel; nothing astounds and all is safe,
   Lightfooted, as once in a lad
   Angel led and dog at heel.
With talent for his pith, fame in his eye,
He makes design and chance, by strength of touch,
   Agree like music on the map
   Of high campaign towards his end.
Then will the Incas blaze near to, like suns.
Rochelle unbend itself.   Madrid give in.
   A prodigy. But in the haste,
   And in the clamour and the sweat,
This sharp acclaim is his own shout, the ray's
Behind his blink of tears: he cannot tell
   That over waste the dawn spilled out,
   The street abandoned when he came.
But I—what I have done has come untied
In spite of all I've tried or said. For long
   I fail. I can do nothing right,
   But heap mistake upon mistakes;
While war's old cart goes slowly creaking on
Into the disillusionary years

Of its real destiny, where later
My own enemy will tread.
Where is my cause, that seems as cold as a blown
Mist? It was so firm, so solid. Must I think
It's I have grown into a ghost?
All is reversed; all is astray;
And reason an old mirror full of flaws.
Gestures that were heroic are remote
As black clouds in a battle-piece;
But they need rain in Barcelona
Where there's blood up to the second storeys.
God of hopes, how you misguide us. We,
Who thought we had the heart and sinews
Of strong beasts, of noble birds—
Head high the running stag, the great in pinion—
Find we emboss, with virtues and with oath,
Only a blason, stony cut,
And which the weathers chip and winds
Chafe. I'd said our coats would boast our pride—
But see, mine's foul and ragged with deceit
Because, by Ronda bridge across
The double cliffs that sheer to drop eight
Hundred feet, and from whose rocks so many
Pigeons flew, instead, the violated
Nuns fall, fluttering.
We thought, this is warm, this is different,
This abscinds us from all past fights, as we marched
among haycocks

With some of the brambles ripe, but the same chill
   Lies on our hair, as in pale winter
   When the saplings are cut through.
Indeed, there's more of torture; and the crime
Of children with their peace hurled into air:
   More fault, more insult and more shame
   Than can be cleaned out from our core—
Unless Time, in its passage round the world,
Should, like an idle workman, make a halt.

✳

When Jacob laid his head upon a stone,
Jacob of Aldgate, he was now alone
In the dear land of Judah. Here the guns
All day had uttered threats like benisons
Over a ground where love and sorrow erred,
As had the prophets that his father heard.
Here was there woe, here desolation came
Advancing long ago, showing her name
Nettles and saltpits and the voice of birds
In empty window-frames: and still could words
Of mercy, lovingkindness, goodness that must
Come, quiver in whiteness like hill dust,
To fade at night time, while through bushes ranged
The small sheep, restless, with their herds, unchanged.
All else is silent. As he turns on rocks
And olive roots, his memory unlocks

Some Reader chanting in a quiet stressed
By pages turned together as a forest
Quickly stirs its leaves; the careful tread
Of carrying the crimson velveted,
The red-wrapped Torah, through a muttered dark
Of men more shy and inward than the Ark;
Or, near the Minories, the hint and fact
Of what man's wits can seize, know, make, transact;
A sale bill of old stock-in-trade across
A dirty shop front; and the grey hurry; gloss
Of rain on pavements; and each market friend
Who stood and joked or argued without end.
These are the last good things he will have known.
For should he live or die, all's twisted and grown
Monstrous from this force of arms; a force
Allowing as much refuge and recourse
As there was bastion or parapet
Against the treachery on Olivet;
A force more harmful than sore ages spent
Burdened by common ache of punishment;
Bringing no gain, nothing redeemable: instead
Blackness and rubble lying over Samson dead.

✡

'I was a Greek. I climbed Aornos' rock for Alexander.
My foot slipped on the pine needles and my breath
    hurt.

Round me men hurtled down to where the Indus
Washes that great crag.'

O men O commanders

'I lived by the Border. Mist would bead our woollen
    cloaks,
Our pelts and faces, on the mornings when we woke
Ready for foraying. I died in the grass
As lonely as a crow.'

O men O commanders

'From Hejaz I. Much I endured of thirst and of sore
    eyes.
I rode for one who led us and for gain, and knew
The camel-thorn, the clefts, the stinging wind
Of promises unkept.'

O men O commanders

'I was a Catalan. I fought in hills near Teruel.
I was so cold and hungry. Who was foe or brother
No one learnt. Black mounds under the snow
Were bodies or else earth.'

O men O commanders

'I a Venetian whom the Genoese strewed on deep
    water.

Spars and oars of all our fleet had snapped like reeds.
I drowned, thinking of young fishermen
Who wade in a lagoon.'

O men O commanders

*

'Here is his picture; you can't see the smile.'
The line of the nose is sad, and the mouth.
'This silver frame is all his monument.'
He looks astonished. That one
Has lowered eyes, as if he knew.

'Sir, the patient has no face, and hears
Nothing.' But the small fitful noise
Of a hill wind is in his ears.

'They must have drifted many
Weeks before they lost hope;
Their bodies had no disfiguring marks
Of oil or sores, but were frayed and bleached
Like an old rope.'

*

Seeing great
Warriors in my head,

And how each yields
His breath in state:
Aruns with mouth against Etruscan asphodel;
The small waves, steeled and glittering,
Of Pompey caught in the shallows;
That stab to Brian, the old king;
Beloved Sir John Chandos on the field
In Vienne, whom the avenging,
Fighting knights can hallow—
I let out my sap,
With sobs, near rotted
Mangold roots that smell
As sour as failure.

✳

Stumbling in retreat,
    The others, still with armed pack,
    Feel flints cut through to their feet,
    Rage at cobbles, curse their knees,
    Thinking they'd been fools to fight.
All's wrecked on either hand.
    We can never talk
    To others: who would understand?
The sight
    Of plough up-ended, spoiled rick,
    Scarecrow in a torn field,
    Is fellow to this fanatic

Whose staring eyes and rigid walk
Keep by me like some dented shield.
How strange, these gables over us and roofs
In blackness where
The rain pours from the guttering,
This splashed filthiness of hoofs.
Cards lie scattered in a tomb.
Someone picks them up and sees
Instead of Queen and Jack,
Hector, Judith and *Lahire,*
Lancelot, Alexandre,
Who should have never left the womb.
French. Throw 'em back.
We hid, we ran, we had
To reach the water; then
Our oars dipped in to make
Eyeless sockets of a crone.
For heaven's sake,
How soon will I be let alone?
Past the thin trees of France,
Or in a wicked wind from side-streets,
Trail a rifle, drag your lance.
Dawn comes up grey and meets
A woman smiling at us, mad;
She puts a finger to her lips,
Shakes her head and slips
Down an alley.
Night will find the bare plain

We captured; there we crawl and press
Through dead ruins of our pain.
My mind's root is bruised: all
I need is nullness
And to lie where I fall.
Everything will be so changed,
I'll feel a clown, the cog
Will never fit, I'll be estranged,
Fears this stalwart who upheld
Enormous courage
In monotony more wasteful
And more weighty than steel wreckage,
And as vacant as the air
Round jealous soldiers' arguments.
A voice has yelled:
Oh God, I dreamt I was where
Women washed our bloodied garments
Out, and looked at us through leafy,
Latticed windows, and were sorry
For us, endlessly sorry.
The last one,
Trudging by his side, is thinking
Of his grizzled dog
At home, with ears aback, blinking,
Old and happy in the sun.

✳

By any men who ever hung on trees
Or who were left, strung over wire,
To turn their heads now this way and now that,
Mire to their knees or groin; and by
The sour weeds on a father's grave;
By nettles grown near outworks of a fort;
By a church buttress which the hurt were laid
Against, their plaints heavy and broken
Like stone draperies of saints—
Never, never again.

By the square, tragic mouth
Of wrath, that may be shameful, hapless,
Or degraded by disaster; and by
Murder done in clean air
And truth wrung out as if a dirty cloth;
By everyone who carried in his mind
Some bright image like a coin,
Yet could not give small change
Or find a right retort, surprised
And piteously;

By any homeless ones who sit,
Emptied of feeling, on a heap of bricks
And grit which was their all;
And chiefly by those who cannot sleep
But—fretting like the wind at night—
Think ceaselessly, had they advanced,

Gone back, been forthright, or declared themselves
Some other time, or place, or way, there would
Have been no utter, endless grief: I swear,
I pray, never again.

PART TWO

MEN AT PEACE

Mist has fallen quietly on air
That once stirred past a mountain fighter's head,
And silent are the rushes where
A boy into Scamander bled.
Hidden in the ground are bane
And warring; and the bitter groans
And orders and the leader's tread
Forgotten in the long rain,
Like little birds that hop among the stones
Of Hebrides and all lapsed islands.

> 'Under the alders
> Just let me be;
> All there is here
> Is drip from alders
> Into a lake
> Of half sunk logs.'

How heavily white fogs
Will roll through fields of memory
To cover pain with northern balm.
Even this Southerner can seldom speak,

Now war is done but, sitting
In his courtyard, listens to the creak
Of chestnut boughs.   Only a leaf will make
A shadow on his wall; the sun
And no one else, can overtake
Thoughts which are too slowly spun
To snare the reason for each hour
Of living, or to understand
Why the clock shows in the tower,
Why the blood beats in his hand.

      'From bed, I hear
      Them sweep the morning's
      Echoing street,
      While the aged maid
      Comes in to set
      The washing ewer
      On a chair.'

Somewhere in a field, there's short grass growing.
With an ear to it, one almost feels
The blades spring. The mind is prone
Or supine, and as calm
As this poor bit of ground
That carries signs of donkey-grazing
And the smells of summer, and that's bound
By a wall so loose and easy-built
That much of it has fallen. Weals

Of many hundred seasons lie
In smallest bract of humble weed or bloom.
But all at once, senses and vision tilt
In shock to the stupendous sky,
Then down, to wonder—could this be the stone
That was once rolled back from a tomb?

> 'O who can bear
> The brass and yells
> That shiver through
> The mended village, while they
> Shoulder flags; it grates
> Against the teeth:
> A blizzard in
> An east wind.'

As Aeneas carried an oar inland,
Knowing the broken coast and pirate ships,
And where they asked him, What's that tool?
He thought it right for a new town to stand;
And as a bird inside a wicker cage,
Kept from all hawking doubt, uncertain rage
Of things, will stretch its feathers to their tips—
So vines may bud; and mirrors fill
With movement; after a trampling from a fool,
Spiders again may sling their webs in dew;
And a rock's outcrop on a hill
Be taken up and cut, as men devise,

For arches to enclose some lengthening view;
While from the lazy meadows spires will rise.

> 'Ted's father, leave
> The graveyard beside the canal;
> Put cap to head
> As you wipe your eyes
> With the back of your hand.
> And you, leave the memorial
> In the dark vault.
> No love dies ever,
> And no fault.'

Free from hateful foreigners—
The way they cut their hair or clear their throat
Or dig their elbows in one's private ribs—each
Is back into his old coat
And usage, land and life:
'Now we can own ourselves, like decent folk.'
In Wales, racked by rivers
Silvering dark lore with rapid speech;
In the scant North, whose men and trees
Make strong and thrifty growth; in Suffolk, flat
As mud, where the slow-voiced have ever spat
From barges beating into estuaries;
Southward, in suburbs growing rife
Between the faces of young plasterers
Or masons handling bricks without a jerk:

Everywhere, these and their jobs of work
Can jogtrot on again like husband and wife.

> 'Contentment's when
> An ache has cleared
> And left us whole,
> While from the borough benches
> Ringing can be heard:
> And Lateran
> Or Lutheran,
> The dear clang
> Breaks into the soul.'

The sea has brought her dowry, and the tide
Has laid its jetsam all along the shore.
But up the hill there's cordial
And beer, new curtains, ashtrays that were coral
Found in a far gulf, and relatives
Crammed closely joking, to admire the bride:
She will be shrewd and practical, and a just
Comfort to this fisherman who must
Tomorrow drag his trawler-nets once more
In rain, on the sea bed.   The sunset gives
The guests, on leaving, music played
Along the crowded esplanade.
And later, a law-copier who lives
On deeds in unstopped verbiage,
Thinks of a past Regatta week,

Rest, and the ferry's shriek,
And sees the crawling wave upon the page.

> 'How civil to dispute
> In neutral air
> Of judges' courts, dusty
> As a sawmill where
> The churning wheel outside
> Clanks in the same place to chide
> Whoever cannot make, assemble,
> Drive and gear together
> Lasting, hard repute.'

*

But here's a morning walked alone
  By someone who, at worst, has known
  Work inside a tutor's book,
  And care, in dry or troutless brook.
  Past glinting bracken of midday
  Where only flies and midges play,
  Past a stone wall, past furzes mean,
  Past a straggle of boreen
  With dusty burrs and beechtree mast
  And fine fir needles on it cast,
  Past tumbling plaint of notes that stop
  Him dead to listen, up at top,
  Past tufted bog, and past the baulk

Of sloe hedge and wet bramble stalk
He goes, to feel the hours that lag
Beside him, run to the fore and drag
His wishes into being filled
With wilds to alter, forms to build.
Soon drafts and invoices are stirred
By the numbed hands of agents in furred
Hats, or else by ledger clerks
Quick tempered in the heat where barques
Ride and part the harbour scum
Outside; till vessels lately come
From Naples or the Baltic Sea
Lean against a Dublin quay
And from their holds pitch out large crates
Of statuary, railings, gates,
Amazon and warrior,
Head of pagan empress, or
Apollo with his sun's horns
That workmen think their Saviour's thorns.
Then for planks and platforms fit
To roll those pedestals of granite
Quarried in his own hills
In which the wind cries out and chills
The nesting plovers of Glencree;
For all must shape as perfectly
As this well-reasoned rockery
Of mosses over grotto's eye
Where, unseen, a trickle learns

Darkness through the dripping ferns.
Ending a path, how curious
  These figures of fierce Eolus:
  Like two great metal men, they blow
  Their curving streams to merge and flow
  Cross-rippled in a bowl; while out
  Of a snub dolphin nose, or spout
  Of lips, more veils of water jet
  To fall in tiers, and then beset
  Slippery shoulders and the charms
  Of nymphs with shells and clutching arms.
Now all's finished, placed and still:
  Nothing base and nothing shrill.
  Here, stone shadows of a cup
  To griffin heads are fluted up;
  Here, acanthus leaves and horn
  Of rams, on urns of bronze are borne;
  Here, in sunk gardens, gods could sip
  At this huge tazza's marble lip;
  While here, the mounting grass succeeds
  Terrace by terrace, till it leads
  To pebbled slopes in black and white
  That imitate each turn and flight
  Where mules go steeply up and down
  And laden, in an Umbrian town:
  Through all, could no more come regret
  Than wild hare with her leveret.
And so, by reed and lake, where the twin

Horses prance in discipline
As, delicate of nose and leg,
They wing the air and seem to beg
Such loveliness to stay, by length
Of alley in the sun's strength,
By each invention and device
That tames the mountains at a price,
You'll wander, and by flickered shade
Of statues in a beech glade,
To let your inmost sadness fall
Blackly, under ilex pall.

✲

So will a voice at random
In the fields become
A structure of compassionate sounds
Which you will climb like ladders in the air,
Until the mighty fugal arguments declare
You noble, sad and great.

So can a nursery play
Of doll, mishap and drum
Grow and then take the boards.
Alone here in a land dream-visited
I breathe a golden day,
And mourn forgotten friends, and wait for the slow
swords
Of my own ancient fate.

So, in a Gothic window,
Virtue with all force must press
In power. Unquenched, the embers glow
Round Peter's robe that's greener than sea deeps;
Saint Eustace aims his shaft as the stag leaps
Through the Cathedral darkness and the dread.

So, if a Londoner,
You go from Amen Corner
Into Paul's, on up under the dome's
Vast hum of silence where the many tongues are
    tomes:
You sit among first books, and read, if you deserve,
Of *Troilus and Criseyde*, how the pen stabs with good-
    ness
And undoes the nerve.

So someone will detect
And map proportions that connect
New threads of reasoning and light
Moving unceasingly in growth, or in the sea's
Suspense, in stars that comb the air with tracks
And problems as with parallax.

So others have preferred,
Through hard resolve and a soft heart, to live
Among the mean and lazy, furtive,
Stupid ones: and to reform the plan;

Or else with hands and brain boldly
To cure the sick: never deterred
By unregenerate man.

So the lens grinder, blest in name, in soul,
In understanding of our load
Of human plight,
And for defining attribute and mode
Of God into one luminous, transparent whole,
Stays gentle and upright.

✲

Such fruit, clamped to the wall,
Fills us till we're gorged,
Or till the rags tear
Or brads bend.
Have we by chance used
Nails the tinkers forged?

✲

For look, philosophers have lungs
That choke on glass-grit, it's been proved;
And children scream; and old men steal,
Or die of cancerous tongues;
We dip slow oars of thought into the night
And find we have not moved;

And what are libraries? Can printed page,
Or even hassock and cold
Stone smelling of piety, assuage
My inner tide of doubt? Light
Is dimmed, the scene rolled,
Smallish dust blows from the stage;
And the dance of a young teague
With casual-cunning toe and heel
Becomes a ponderous Germanic gigue;
And where, by twisted fountain and by ways
So devious and delighting that the running gaze
Was lost, enchanted, in the sight—yet
 The very stillness of the air's a fret,
A hint, a whisper of the growing
Need for some harsh harrowing.

✳

A room where arguing intellectuals whine,
Then limply give their hand and start again;
Another, where the Adam style pilasters
Echo with the self-important cough
Of old and knuckle-rubbing men who like
The softly lapping fire, the rustled *Times*,
After a hard day's hunting: those who once
Had felt at home in either, are aghast.

We'll go no more to the woods, they're now bricked up
And villas grow as campion by the way;

And all along wet tarmac hoardings show
In boredom, like the new and cleanly pub;
And a mock Tudor tea-house mocks itself,
Mocks hunger, and the fools who think that beams
And pewter jugs and cakes are carrying
Them daintily into a turbid past.

We'll walk instead on pavings and on paths
Where grass is trodden and the elms are tamed,
And dogs, the smart-trimmed and the common dogs,
Play in the Parks, and small boys pitch their stumps,
And tramps unwrap things from a newspaper,
And women mince, and prams are wheeled along
For ever, under careless sweeping clouds
To the far roar of buses round about;

Or, from a City roof, we'll see how soot
Lies in the flowerpot left on a sill;
How iron rusts; and the eroded bricks
Rise up in grimy insult to the air,
Whichever way they're set; and humans live
As bindweed grows over a clinkered mound—
Here, and at back of equal towns whose streets
Such windows scan, while never a face looks out.

For now our thoughts are caught in thicket growth
Which slowly strangles them with age; they feel
Mute as the woollen horns, fixed as the chase

In darkened forests of some tapestry
Which has been stared at, for no purpose, for
Too long; being as stale and as exhausted
As the parlour walls, and yellow air,
And ticking clock, of all dead afternoons.

We have turned back from Tragedy, that land
Of warning and of storms and godlike speech
Upbraiding us, griping our mind and marrow,
As in winter, trunks of trees seem twisted
One way by a giant's hand—gone back
To comic papers, and euonymus,
The promenade, and sandfleas on the beach,
And strum and tinkle of the blackface coons.

Once, in the dark of obsequies, our passion
Thickened till it grew to total might;
And once in childhood, over the wall: and there
The river's shining promise in the meads;
But now, as salesmen moving through half lights,
We're like tired women walking under trees
Of rainy suburbs, on uneven heels,
In ugliness, unkindness and in waste.

Meanwhile, through institutions towering
Like their unending, shadowless grey days,
There's been amassed in record, ledger, file
And down long office corridors of fact,

Index and tabulation of our deeds,
So that all things are noted and exact,
Balanced, budgeted and accounted for—
Except that life seems pointless and disgraced.

*

By all ruined learning,
Where it may be:
By saint that spoke
On small isle's space
Whose silverweed
Now meets the sea;
And Glendalough
Where oar's stroke
Guides the tripper
Through deep rest
And quiet face
Of hermit's creed;
By systems of grace;
The good in all things
Confused as talk,
Or stray as goats
In cemetery
Of Muslim bones;
Priests cramming
The crumpled notes
In a case, who say

'You'll make it up later';
And Jews caught
In the Law's decay,
Who stuff their prayers
In cracks of stones
At the Temple's base;
By Christ so crippled
From what's been taught,
He calls for a crutch
And tries to walk;
And by each empty
Site in the heart
Once great, yes,
As Armageddon
Was when manned
And walled apart,
But stared at, now,
Quite openly—
I know how much
Has fallen, how
Akhnaton's mildness
Slid like sand:
Oh, lights are showing
In Guildford, and people
Are yawning for tea.

*

Whoever is in low
Relief, faintly embossed,
Take heed, take care,
For you will be erased.
No more is noon when the groom shaves,
Peace under trees, or safety
The gilt vanes of Penshurst
In the sun. But time
And place are strewn
With cloud, lost like fumes
Within a darkness fit
For burning rubbish,
And the knife's release:
It lops what's done
To let new growth swell out.
O that I'd bud and break
And truly live—for look,
What heroes make us proud:
Such as refuse, deny,
And with perverted strength
Draw back, or those
Who most abundantly
And warmly breathe, and use
Their love, and swear, and fight
Into the press of things?
Find me a cause
Or a catastrophe
To crack and shake the false,

The phrased, the laggard pleas
Of a restraining clause.
For now, thank God, no more
Dismayed by Death—
(I blushed to think of her,
Froze in the night, and held
My breath)—I'll fondly give
My seamless skin and know her,
Like a man.

PART THREE

WOMEN IN LOVE

Clearly as a fife and drum
   Down the village lane may come,
   As bells may suddenly be hurled,
   Or willow and the ash be swept
   Into greying gusts of fear,
   As it rains, as starts the wren
   Or shyly mannered maiden wept:
   So is caring ever near,
   Ever hidden, as the death
   Of squirrel by a root; and we
   Who watch a woodman split a tree
   To its pale heart, at any breath
   May feel love with one heavy blow
   Cleaving us from head to toe.
   Then life and the whole sky turn chill
   And set us shivering, as when
   Europa, with her friends at play
   In hot sweet sultry fields, away
   By the great creamy bull was led
   Along a bitter shore, until
   Her hair was lifted by the wind
   And over the dark ripples sped
   The two to rough-topped Crete.

Even the ageing, the wise-eyed,
  The disenchanted women; those
  Most unassailable whose prose
  Of peace is round them like a dress;
  Even the unforgetting ones
  Who'd let no further pain compress
  Their lives; and those whose memory
  Is faded like a token saved—
  (That letter or that strand of hair
  Which has lost all its power and sense;
  As, on a wall, a sword can hang
  Quite disregarded, yet engraved
  With battle honours of the past,
  And rust eats out what was immense)—
  They'll feel its touch; and those who've tried
  To act like vagabonds dispersed
  In public gardens, through May's hush
  Will find the dark red hawthorn flush
  And warmth, will know the pang and fear
  Of couples that year after year
  Shelter beneath it, stand in thrall
  Without a word, and wait for the first
  Thunder drops to fall.

Exalt this giant cloud, this clash,
  This storm that shakes our inmost being,
  Cracks foundations, and discovers—
  In the instant of a flash—

That what was old is fresh and strange;
Exalt the boldness and delight
Of finding that if in our lover's
Eyes we stare, on shafts of light
Like will, like sight, like air we range
To every landscape of the feelings,
Every climate of the temper:
To an innocence of mornings
Milky new, without a name;
Or among dust and tracks that bring
Us nearer to some ancient fame;
Or to the icy wind and mountain;
To a Cappadocian plain
Where monks, in emptiness of heat,
On rocks rasp their hems and feet;
To the wild places; or to ease
Of rivers; or contemptuous seas:
In turbulence and risk.

For watch: wherever someone grieves,
As on a terrace along which
Scatter and skelter the dry leaves;
Or on a foggy waterfront;
In shops; or in the City square
Whose starlings clatter by the thousand
While at open windows, working
Typists fill the answering air;
In every time and place and land

(Perhaps they've known the other stress
Of stoical foolhardiness,
But this time without heaume or casque,
Sallet or helmet, as in war
Their men—and they—had worn before)
Do women, unremarked, alone,
Stroking their forearm absently,
Or most composed and easy, ask
Only for the might, the nerve
To love (for God's sake don't be grateful),
To agree, give tribute, serve,
Perish, and bear the brunt.

*

Where is the lumber-room of what was important?
The bric-a-brac of old feelings? Finished, put away.
And where the motes of ideas we breathed for our *now*?
Lost corridors, stray paths in the woods to our *here*?
Forgotten, of no account. In me, I feel
New space, new time, strangely careened and on whose
Axes spin my world, as you and I—
The man, the woman—tremble face to face.
The air is filled with power, hesitancy,
And awareness sharp as a blade's edge:
The lightest gesture, the least sign, can alter
Our whole fate.   Opposed like this, we know,
We two, the other's soul is the most threatening

And immediate fact there's ever been—
You are so whole and real, he says, and keeps
Back tears; she, Nothing can stop the force
Of this great hour. I, as a woman, know
That from this confrontation such momentous
Grace or plight will come, it is the reason
I was born peasant in the rain
Or one who trails her mantle in the hall;
That centuries have waited and prepared—
Rehearsing with mimed passion and mock battles—
For this one and overpowering cause:
A cause whose glare lights up the skies and roofs,
Streets, spires, alleys of the mind
With an intensity so sacrificial
That its blazing flash and burning shadow
Fill with unseen, heroic acts. What
Can profane, he thinks, such faith as this? And she:
In finding you, I find myself, will cry.

For now I understand all twofold things;
How dark and light, matter and spirit, gut
And brain can be acquainted, how they accord:
Angel and beast in me are one: because
The midway heart is held between
What's private, base, and what's diffused and rare,
Binding the two as the sun's power can weld
The soil, where his foot rests, into quick life
With upper levels of the air. Through me

All contraries of grief and joy are strung:
I am rage and mercy, impulse and slow patience,
Folly and wisdom; I am the rain-filled wind,
The blade that suffers drought. I've tolled
A bell of duty harshly; groaned and wept
For mercy like a saint on a stone floor.
One fears me, and of one I go in terror;
I am those Fates with scant hair and red eyes
And brittle bones, who so disdain the young;
I am the thread that stretches to be nicked.
I am a parody and extreme, but round me
All natural things are stupid, without substance:
People with idiot faces, in nameless houses,
Going on errands that can have no meaning.
Aloof from others, I still speak for them
And must fulfil them. Bending my ear to catch
The oracle, at the same time it's I,
Fume-crazy croaking sibyl, who predict it.

In full process, now, of secret planning,
Anguish and boredom—and again anguish, all the time
Feeling his presence and voice: at night when all's
    quiet,
During the racking day, but chiefly in crowds
Where I always think I have found him, or see some-
    one like him—
Each faculty and each nerve (for he tests me in every
Thing at all moments), each vigour is taut, alert,

Made into a halter for triumph which now almost
 gentles
Up to my hand and then, will slip away;
Each fibre throughout my frame is used, with enough
Force and guile to wrench away an empire,
Or to exhaust the world with strategies.

✻

Should anyone ask, Where are these battlefields?
Perhaps in the country house
Where a clammy mist falls over the garden,
Fills muddied lanes
And surges into the guest room.

Perhaps in some Park.
Municipal ducks, freezing lake,
Reeds like straw,
And an old bottle caught in the ice.

Perhaps by sand near prickled,
Sea-pitted coral rocks,
Where fond hope and insufficiency
Are the same as anywhere else;
While in the heat
Roads blind you with whiteness.

These are my Flanders, Valley Forge, Carthage.

✻

Principles are my breath,
They fly like vapour from my mouth:
O I am mad mad
As whorls of air round hills, as air
From shining cold of mountains
Tumbling to warm itself over
The breast of plains, turning
In branches of the carob tree,
Then seeking shade and grace
Under a marble bridge, a causeway;
Or as harlot water
Feeling, always moving, among
Palaces whose stone has
Stepped its weight into my arms.
My breathing is the raucous
Laughter and the clatter from
A Venetian supper-tent
Whose awning stripes billow to noise
And negro-carried wine
Sways where they order feasts and fountains:
Not those droplets arching
Neatly in a spaced design
Of careful gardens, but
Untamed exuberance of limbs
Shaken by Erzulie;
Or Gold Coast heat and sweat filled
With birdcalls, thickness of tropic
Scent, and fire from scarlet flowers

Whose leaves must creep and thrust
And spike and choke each others' lives—
This air inspires me now.

*

I said inspired: fully
    I mean it. Each word,
Each event, shows me its own,
    Natural tact;
From chance, or proper command,
    I am the elect.
My devotion is felt as it walks
    Beside the young preacher
Who once climbed up to the pulpit,
    A rose in his mouth—
And look how confidence
    Can lie in my hand
That's loose and open, power
    Along my arm
Smoother than lip of a shell;
    And how my gladness
Breaks the sea in spurts
    Of dolphin foam.
How easy to move, to act!
    Forebodings have fled
As bat-form shreds of cloud
    Escape at sunrise;

What was difficult
  Is plain as noonday
Heat in light that dazzles
  The lost marshes
Over which our thoughts
  Shake in the air
Like larks: this light, strong
  As was the vision
That Aquinas saw
  And then fell silent
To dispute no more,—
  Giving us glory,
Lustre, unity,—
  Wakens the Future
From half-lidded sleep:
  Who, with his eyes
Near blinded by behests
  And glare, shuts them,
Deciding to impose
  The shadow of old
Doubts, policies,
  And debts again.

Within our curtained alcove
  We are so near
To stab each other: deeps
  Of uncertainty
Must hang between our heads.

My destiny,
And yours, swing up and down
   In scales that give
No justice, only judgment;
   While we watch
Grave statements rise like dust
   Of war, havoc
From messages that stray,
   Fears from a freshly
Toppled plan; and then
   Observe disjunction,
Incoherence, lack
   Of sense: with pity
And the ancients' terror
   On our face.

*

'As through the field
Walked I and my true lover,
I did discover
Goodness in gateways heeled
By cattle, dreams in the meres
And hope in taste of clover.
Now all I need
Is to forget,
For since our quarrel

78

All in the world's a weed,
And tears are salt as sorrel.'

✳

That slightest shiver of wind
  Before dawn is the shock
To my soul when it learns he has ceased,
  Yes, ceased, to care.
Which blunder have I made,
  Where was I wrong,
To be shown that miracles
  Are past? What
Have I done, for retribution
  To come on me swiftly,
Savagely and teach me
  That fortitude
Is no use and cannot prevent
  My being destroyed?
'Pourrvou que cela dourre . . .'
  Had said a mother,
Bending to blow her nose
  In the Corsican gutter.

I bit into the day
  To find it rotten;
Would I could spit it out.
  Recriminations,
Bitterness, reproach,

Have opened a gulf,
Have cracked Time in two—
  Time that in splendour
Of success elided
  Into long
Negations of itself;
  Time that could be
Timeless, without front,
  Without direction,
Pace or guidance; mixed
  Until those Persian
Arrows blackening
  The sun, and children
Who feared dusk, were one;
  A Time fed
By many equal founts,
  So that the chirp
And clink and chattering
  Of Spring was twin
To shrivelled sycamore
  And the wet leaf
Of amber-dropping lime.
  But now, sharpest
Calamity has cut
  Its marks all round me:
Painful and precise,
  Their steps and minutes
Cleave and allocate.

It's thought the Angel
Said to the first woman:
   'Now, walk slowly
From the garden, slowly,
   For perhaps
You will be called back.'
   But God has despised me,
I am no longer watched,
   My thoughts guessed,
Giving anxiety, care,
   Giving alarm:
But ignored. This is defeat
   Unalterable,
This is the worst, the most
   Unrelenting revenge.

✻

The wet wind storms the branches
And trees shake; the same wind,
   Blowing where there are boats,
Jumps them against the mooring ropes.
   Unless the tree uproots,
Or the rope breaks, or I go mad,
   There is no leaving. When
I see him who has this contempt of me,
   I feel a hot wave of sickness
Then quickly, cold despair. I think

How surely and easily
Could I have still held my advantage,
  Had I said this or done that;
And dreams recur, showing some new
  And splendid mastery
To give my pride a triumph in daylight,
  Instead of it cringing, begging,
Along tenebrous streets of the mind
  Where arch and girder are broken
And behind the dignity, degradation is seen,
  And stupidity, emptiness.
The friends of bereaved cities feel shame
  To look at them, they find nothing
Noble or great in devastation
  Of what was once entire.

*

She ran from the vast house and her pheasant shooting
    brothers
Towards the light there was in learning, towards
    living.
Amused, eccentric, kind; a witty ghost, warm soul
And mighty to understand, slowly she'd speak or move
Or give her arm and look into the eyes of those
Entranced by her, to find (so her whole life, she hoped)
The superb effulgence, the total intimacy of two
 Feeling minds. Most of them mocked her afterwards.

She was heroic. She died alone in herself as always.
The London pigeons wheeling in wind and traffic, the
    pressure
And pressmen at the church door, or inside: she was
    nowhere in this.

A second one's young, and as she's walking down the
    street
Whose windows all of them have ferns in brass pots
And elderly ladies at desks answering their letters,
Her swimming eyes are remembering collegiate leaves.
She can discern no raddled cheeks, no sagging body
Of some collapsed Fury, no terror through her calm,
As she passes these victims of double dealing, or of
    powerful
Respectability, these reprobates and bullies, examples
Of bores, or what is raffish, pompous or calculating.
She thinks the worst her dreams can ever do to her
Is fail to show a mask of leaves, a crumbled urn.

A third one sees her tended, heavy-scented garden
From the verandah. A dog yawns. A cage swings.
Not a blister of paint, not a spiderweb, not a branch
    out of trim,
Not a blemish on a waxed table, not a dab of dirt in
    the kitchen—
And yet, under this bland and meticulous order, the
    blister,

The shaking thread, the disbalance, the blame, the
    horror are hidden
But always in mind. It's fifty years since there was a
    man
Who strolled and whistled, quick and carefree, like the
    whipping waves,
Whom she would have gone with, now as then, any-
    where—
To a strange land with the wind rattling the window
    panes.
'Come on, dogs; well, little bird?' and her hand
    trembles.

                ✳

        I can see
        Berenice dragging her robe
        Between bare pillars
        From the sun;
        Heloise a nun
        Still unconsolable;
        Kind Dorothy enduring
        Mist and rocks
        Colder than those of Cumberland;
        And Mary sweet as phlox;
        While Harriet has a scent
        Of water's edge
        Where now the pert

And nervous mallard and teal
Are watched by Parkgoers
From a gravelled ledge
In air that's brisk and fluent.
But for my loss of heart,
My pain,
There's a tapping
Window blind, or
A muddle of rain.

*

Let me slip away or sleep
Or die. How can I go back
Into each day's
Queasy remembering?

I envy the very old
With their faces wiped clean
Of moods and movement;
No pulpy flesh under the skin:
Only a covering for the skull.

Indoors, there's always a smell
Of stale affirmations,
Of yesterday's gala
And its unswept floor.

Outside, leaves have fallen.
  Branches squeak and rattle
  Over the empty pavilion
  Where we acted, and over
  The rusting music-stands.

Women who are silent in manner,
  Or wildly frivolous, or crazy,
  Or dispirited, or merely aimless
  And vague—do I seem one of them?

The ravaging
  Use of feeling and valour;
  All the uncommon goodness
  That's been spent,
  Laid waste.

Look at the tattered room
  Exposed to the sky.
  No splendour in this ruin,
  But shame in small wallpaper
  For all eyes.

We were bright beings
  Made of wave and plunging light:
  In the surprising seas we sauntered
  Who now dry our dirtied nets
  Upon the rocks.

The hot reminders
   Of what's gone: the cold revulsion
   From what's done.

The mind is open,
   Desolate, swinging in the wind
   Like a knocking gate;
   While autumn woods all smoulder
   Till put out by rain
   And pigeons clip the empty air.

                    ✻

There's nothing
For an edifice. Not even
Such small figurines of clay
As are found in a tomb on the hillside:
Children, shawled and capped,
Carrying sheaves and dancing.
No weight is left, no tenderness,
As on a sarcophagus lid
Where man and wife lie knee to knee,
His bracelet twining on her wrist,
His marble fingers
Curving round her arm.

                    ✻

By our crawling
Spaniel-race;
By pitchfork prongs
Of remorse that pierce us
And toss us about
Like mice in the straw;
By brutish things
To shudder at: snouts
Grunting at Circe,
Gaze of wrong
From mottled venom-face;

By the stretched tendons
Of the two robbers;
By him who thanked
Or scolded each person
More deeply than soul
Ever since or before;
By the women who stood
Beside those nailed planks—
We who spoke low
Under our hoods—
For pity's sake, no more.

PART FOUR

WOMEN AT PEACE

Round my whole mind, the same
And snowy landscape lies
That once came with its blank
On Tobit's worried eyes
And gently covered up
His troubles. Earth is sealed.
Dead still the staring-coated
Bullocks in the field.
Stiff is each reed, each twig
Unmoved, each trickle stopped,
Unuttering, and seized
With numbness where it dropped.
Level and like all things,
Which way I turn my head,
With only a hunched bird
To show there's roof or shed
In country as well known
To me as home. But should
The scene thaw out, and I
Then wander by a wood
Or undergrowth of coppice

Fenced with ash, by farms set
Tightly in the weald,
By empty branches' net—
Still will the leaden road,
The sky, the death of sound,
The slaty cold and dumbness
Keep my senses bound
As in a trance—until
One morning when I wake,
Wake suddenly, not knowing
How, not knowing why,
Feeling a change to climates
Nearer South . . .

*

Clear, clear
Like a young cockerel's cry,
The singing of a boy
Along a hill.
I listen,
Free as this easy air
So thin, so clean.

In the dark grove
Of mandarini trees
Under my window,
Snicking clacking gardeners

90

Take up the snatch of tune:
They curl it, turn it
And repeat it till it's twisted
Like the under-branches
They are cutting.
After that,
A little raking.

No more
To be watched
By high and hungry gods,
But to feel light, drained;
To move about as I wish;
To get beyond this garden
To the wild slope.

Lying in its grass,
All I can hear now
Is someone smacking a carpet
Far off, beyond the water tanks,
And very faintly
Children's cries.

There's no more need
To run aslant the world.

✳

Meanwhile, elsewhere: 'I don't care
A kick of a hen,' says this one.
'The cold clank of the bucket handle,
The rat running on the wall,
My mother who hasn't a step in her since
She broke her thigh, the turf-smoke
And my face concealed in it—
All these are good enough.'

Another: 'Let us stop heroic
Lies and allegory. Too many
Statues have baton and blank eyes
Directed over the market-place;
Even the emblems—eagle, winged lion—
Of Evangelists, fail
To convince me: I prefer
A plover in a field,
The cat curled in a grocer's shop.'

The waves of Galilee have furled
Rose-imaged oleanders
For an age. Along the shore
Magdala, a mud village with fowls,
Has forgotten Mary. Women
Now help deepen rough red furrows,
Making a heritage,
An orchard crop, for boys and girls

Pale-haired under this sun
Instead of dark as ghettoes.

Each day is dependable and
Controlled, like an office clock; steady
As some figure with black skirt
And black umbrella you see move
Among glass bells where Bon Chrétien
Blanches the rain of Paris suburbs.
Reason, in charge of itself, craves
To build new colonnades of thought,
Or prove a spangle-lit
Fresh spark of theory, or free
Old proverbs from the humped tels.

＊

If one could see beyond house fronts
Into the past, as through a pane
Of glass, the tremendous roar, then quiet,
Of dying in rubble would be plain.
But beams and bricks are up again.

Under Crimean harbour depths,
What silent traffics go between
Sunk Greek galleys, green swaying weed
On marbles of the Chersonese,

Out-of-date warships, rebel cruiser,
Engine parts of every kind
And bones odd sizes—all of these
Washed like cockles of the sea?

In streets where paper blows about,
A stab goes through me of the talk
That brought disastrous happenings,—
The death of feeling that I caused.
Urchins playing give a shout
And the thought leaves me as I walk.

*

Gone is anything sick, sad or fanciful.
What moved me was the hand of the Mechanized
    Chessman,
Horror and mystery in his stuffy robes.
What I've been through was the Hall of Mirrors,
Distorting mirrors of a fair. What I've seen
Were obscene freaks in a sawdust pit,
And scenes painted with size, swollen
The size of hallucinations—
All believed in at the time,
All suffered as one suffers
The anaesthetic dream
Of spiritual blessedness,

Of spirals choiring:
Then afterwards,
The fit of weeping.

*

There's a small hill on the Bog of Allen
With jackdaws and beeches and a square house.
The maids are by the fire. They sew and speak
Of a cousin, or how to help the niece,
Or will Dolan sell, or of the boy
One of them went with (as she bites a thread),
Or else the time long back when they found
An empty can of tea and some sandwiches
Wrapped up in a *Freeman's Journal*, and left
By the ambush there must have been at the gates
(And the mistress in bed seeing on the wall
The flash of the fired barracks across the way);
And will her great-grandchildren, they wonder,
Take after their da?

It's to be hoped they will,
Thinks their mother (keeper of all things
Who has watched her children sleep) who now watches
    them
With her husband making a garden bonfire.
He's grinning and swearing under his breath
And tearing his coat and telling them how to help.

95

Screaming, happy in doing something
And bringing the wrong sticks, they'll now and again
Take fright at the blaze, run away to her, then
Forget and dash back to add more. She looks
At their napes, at the back of their knees, and sighs:
How to guard them from danger, from fear,
For ever? The dogs go off to sniff and to hunt
On their own. Smoke tingles and eddies
Through sparks of laughter, gusts of seriousness
That are insubstantial and flickering
To anyone else—but to her, solid
And round as the brick oasthouse in the yard.

*

Leaf upon earth, and loam under the frame,
And pear, espaliered, nailed across a wall;
The chatter of small-territoried birds,
Or a staked plant that where it blooms will fall;
The fly crawling up a stem it hugs;
Beetles that drag their carapace, alone,
Intent, through thickest grass where groundbees drone;
A swan that dents her breast against an edge
Of lake, her feet now softly on the ooze
And now her bill nudging in roots of sedge—
These are my kin (she well might cry), their labours
Are my days and reasoning: as strong

And logical as Schoolmen after long
Disorder, wreckage and dark anarchy.

＊

We will now do the linen. The weight of it, lifted out of
    deep drawers
    And cool to the touch, and the warm smell when it's
    taken
    Out of the airing cupboard, give me a pride
That any woman has felt who's putting a room to
    rights,
    Scrubbing as if herself were being scrubbed,
    Scouring as if her soul were being scoured,
Straightening up and sorting as if in her own mind.
    (My helper, bending her neck, shows tendrils of hair
    That surely her friend, who has his bicycle propped
This instant against the ivied wall, admires.   Let him
    wait.)
    Each household has its manner and proper speed
    For seeing to this or preparing that. How good
To spice and flavour well; to walk the dim and white
    And dairy-smelling passages; to look
    From any window on to broad lands,
Or on to harbours when the fishermen are home
    (Their boats are EVIE II and MARIA SOCCORSA
    With dories slung on the pilot-house roof, the snow
Filling them)—to be safe, and have enough for the fire.

Or beside other quays where in markets, we women,
Scarf-faced and red-fingered, must sell fish:
This is also good, the mist mingling with our breath
In gossip and curses, to rid us of old shames
And old mistakes that make us groan at night.

*

Crones stop in the street and mumble
    In each others' faces;
    Their grandsons are masons perched
    And painting overhead;
    Their nieces are washerwomen
By stones of some broad rivermouth
    Dried to a middle trickle.
    In a room with drawn blinds
    Loneliness is consoled
    Between covers of the Bible:
Often you only have to grasp
    The book to feel worthy.
    D'you notice how old women
    Who have missed a destroying
    Happiness look away?
Whereas the old and plain who meet
    Your eyes, do so because
    They know they are more holy,
    Or else more powerful—
    Even if they've acquired

A look of snapped twigs, or hollow
    Beetle-sherds, or gnawed
    Husks, or have about them
    A faint, discernible smell
    Of mouldering earth and deadness.

But growing girls: slow airs
Of cowslip warmth blow from you.
    Some, whose pairs
Of breasts are tightly met
Together as young apples,
    Will perhaps get
Caught by gasp and relish
Of mock struggle, and
    Become a prudish
Housewife or a drudge or
Slattern. You, the rest—
    Whatever your
Demeanour, epoch, dress
And voice, timid or dowried
    Ones no less
Than waif or heroine—
Are sisterly to those
    Who moved in muslin
On a tender lawn;
Who left the art-room, its chill
    Casts undrawn;
Outgrew a corridor

Of pianos practising
In muffled war;
And who forgot the yew
As hiding-place. Your state
Is strange, new,
Unhurried as the run
Of angels, neither ended
Nor begun;
Your thought the shape and shade
Of soft air through a marble
Balustrade:
Untried and unexpressed,
You wish for marvels, danger,
Deeds unguessed.

*

If I could be like Niobe,
Mother of many, before the vengeance,
My robes brimming out with goodness,
Filled with content . . . But I cannot.
Something weak and nagging in me
Causes me to turn my head,
After a time, at any noise
Coming from far off, carried
By the wind from places where,
If you're in trouble, the old whore
And the old soldier, blunt, blowsy,

Plain as plain, are to be utterly
Trusted; where philosophies
Are arguments it's best to forget
Or else to remake each hour, and feel
Alter with a change of light,
With new work started, or the sound
Of sudden wet, below, in the street.
Lately, I notice that the flattened
Saints no longer burn their windows
But are idle and remote;
And I can't bear to watch the winter
Smokiness on playing-fields;
Or poverty, like a goat in its range
Over the common, along the waste:
And though ill-humour and a certain
Haste now hover in the air,
The day dangles an empty bridle.

*

'Hidden in the womb I lie
With beating heart and closed eye,
Thinking forward, casting back,
Through our living almanac.
Covered in as warm a tide
As this, and lapped from side to side,
I was washed in altered forms
By huge calms and vaster storms

Of that primal, misty sea
Tasting of futurity.
Gone my gills—but see their cleft—
Long before the Alps were left
Higher than the lakes which fell
Into gloom of bitter spell.
I have been near scale and quill,
Furry chine is with me still;
Seen the rocks and plains dissolved,
Seasons, heavens, aims resolved;
I have reaped bread from a weed;
Searched to find out every need
Of my horror or my trust,
Ecstasies, constraint, disgust
And rebellion. Fortified
By great portents, I have tried—
Using all my brain and force,
All my will, all my resource—
To build a wall up in between
Good and evil. I have been
Vain as cities, poor as hills,
Travelled through such endless ills,
Through such hope and fear and rage
For an unremembered age,
That I beat my prisoned fist,
Angered that when I untwist
From this closeness into air
Final and fulfilling, there

I must barter, prate and mime
For a pulse, a blink of time.'

*

How we hate each other
In a narrow room,
   We terrible knitters
   Under the lamp;
How we knot and lace
The hours interminable,
   Intricate and
   Pale as in
The Book of Kells, we nuns
And all unmothers of men;
   Or we who look
   At backs of houses
As we sit and stitch,
Crowded elbow to side,
   Handling the stuff
   And stiff brocade
Of death: for that is how
It seems to us who stifle
   Here, bound
   By a weight of days;
How we regret not seeing
Leaves in an approaching
   Storm fly up;

And how we envy
All of those who rustle
In such silks, and thread
   Their words with looks
   Brilliantly false,
By chandeliers, the tinkle
And the palms, before
   They praise, thank,
   And yawn to bed.

＊

Solomon kept chariot horses
Stabled under Temple walls.
They stamped within their hollow stalls.

I must escape, I must avoid
The puckered mouth and twitching thumb
Of Age who waits for me to come.

Swifts flicker round the sill,
Beat their shadows on the blind,
Beat their hurry in the mind.

＊

She has reached
The rim of time
The dune end

Of the world.
Spiked grass
Loose sand
What to lean on
Where to turn . . .
Something recalled
Before it is known,
Old as the ground
New as herself
But sharp and steep
As memories
Of crag and shelf
In witless sheep
Who make a mountain
Track on lowly
Downs, of rushing
Winds in birds
Who now are placid
On the green
But once were wilder
Than the air—
Some voice in her
That tries to find
And utter the old
Chants, the old
Pain, cries out:

✳

O random Fate, who rout
And shatter and unbind
The elbow-leaning, tame,
Demurest pieties—
Free me that I may wear
A yoke I hanker for
And name: precise belief
In the authority
And overbearing deeds
Of a loved mortal, one
Whose strength and tongue shall be
The provenance of right;
A part in all transactions
Of his mind and any
Tragedies which follow.
Admit that the devout
Must have sanction from Church,
A thief from others' failings,
The privileged from custom,
Scholar from book—and I
From discipline of great
And terrible truths. Hold me,
Pour back my soul, let me know
Life the unfinished: so
Reflood the desolate ebb:
Renew me, make me whole.

From 'A Cloud Across the Sun' (1949)

FOUR MEN'S DESIRE

John the Baptist stood with hair
Blown through by the morning air.
Calloused, lean as thorns and brown,
Over the bare land and down
The listening ear of time he spoke
A prologue nothing can revoke.

John, the son of Zebedee,
From the sweet Tiberian sea
With its kingfishers and quail
And oleanders, rips the veil
Of laziness. Through streets the crowd
Argues with him strong and loud.

John, asleep at Ephesus,
Stir your jaws and pray for us!
Faint for love, we tread the ground
As pilgrims on a holy mound,
Waiting to be subtly kissed:
O preacher and Evangelist.

John of Patmos, round your isle
Waves clash and suns beguile
As you mouth, with roughened lips,

A barbarous Apocalypse—
Great visions of a lunatic
Or a world convulsed and sick.

First, the vague prophetic sounds
Usher truth that yet astounds;
Then a contemplative love
Transcends what any deed can prove:
If last, disintegration's fire
Should come, Earth knows four men's desire.

IRELAND

This is the country
That has no desolation, no empty feel
(The pagan kings are always there)
In ruined abbey, ruined farmhouse,
Slab of cromlech, or a wheel
Travelling a bog road
Through Calary's too quiet air.

NO ENTRY

When Hector's foot comes creaking on a stair,
Or Helen's breath steams in the frozen air:
Moments that no one ever sang:
These are the hidden places where

I move about and find
    Some freshness for the mind,
  A gap to be explored with care,
As over David's harp in a dark corner
Runs a mouse and gives it a small twang.

Constricted space! Others, I know, have wide
Imaginary fields where they confide
    Their dreams and where they roam at ease—
    For little Hamnet hasn't died,
        But makes a swing with other
        Children; look, Leander
    Steps out backward from the tide—
Not only dreams but systems of escape
As furious or everyday as these:

She's thin and sallow. The headmistress pays
Her meanly to curb the English pupils' ways:
    Tenez-vous convenablement.
    Outside, a château park decays
        With drifting leaves, in spite
        Of drifting girls . . . Then flight
    To her room—the *Nuit de Mai*—to gaze
At the full-bosomed Muse, the poet's brow
And welling sadness—*Ah, quel ravissement!*

Young Ted, the garden boy, unsmilingly
Will trench and stake and dig. I'll lay a ready

Bet he'd never swear or fight—
With summer hanging heavily,
    Or autumn smelling sour,
    When colder winds scour
The earth, or shoots break out. Instead he
Glows, he burns from direst sin's repentance
While he shouts and moans on Chapel night.

That tramp, dirty as the London soil,
Hugs a Park bench, his hideous face a foil
    To children, birds and dogs, whose scufflings
    He's too motionless to spoil.
        Let the weak winter sun
        Show the tree's skeleton,
    The sharp leaves' scurry and recoil,
And daze his red-rimmed eyes and part his lips
As peace swoops to him on her pigeon wings.

Or other ways of sidling, groping back
From the affront of living. Almanac,
    Great pyramid and portent turn
    The sluggard-rolling zodiac
        Into 'What month, dear, were
        You born?' and 'Now it's clear:
    We add . . .' The invisible tide is slack
And lost Atlantis silent; but those ears
Catch auguries which drown them in concern.

Even the Libyan Arabs take retreat
To their Green Mountain, up a thousand feet,
　　Their grazing lands. But I'm shut out:
　　No entry, even by deceit;
　　　　Not with my eyes clamped tight
　　　　Against the speckled night;
　　And never in my work, whose beat
Hurts with its knock and actual daily pulse
Of stinging joy, short ease and constant doubt.

ANY TROUBLED AGE

O mussel coloured houses by the dunes
With fluttered boats feeling among the shoals,

　　How many times can it have happened,
　　How many times

O mountain straked and softened by blue air
With trickles fingering between the reeds,

　　How many times can it have happened,
　　How many times

O cottage field warmed by the breath of sheep
When rain begins to gossip in the hedge,

　　How many times will woman see
　　Some man trudging

To the door, and rise, with a broken welcome—
For the whole news has travelled in his eyes.

ALTER EGO

Mephisto and the Wandering Jew,
Ghost and gombie, witch and hoodoo:
 These are a tin cat-head
 Trembling on a thread
To frighten birds! The devil's brew
That does exist, stirs in you.

No malediction neared your crib;
Yet underneath the vaulted rib
 And flip-flap of your lungs,
 Darkly as in dung's
Warmth, there breeds and grows the glib
Cruelty that moves a nib,

Beats a dog, aims a gun,
Maims the Father, kills the Son,
 Infects a realm, and haunts
 The body with such taunts
And horrors that you shriek Be done . . .
I know, for you and I are one.

ARCHITECTURAL TOUR

A pillar wrecked
By sand; the slat
Of softest leaves
To hide a voice
And hint its echo;
Pediments
Where hogmaned ponies
Prance in fat
Of stubbornness;
Or the stones
Of Clonmacnois,
Lichen-flecked;
Cupolas that
Burst through snow;
Spires where angels
Catch their gowns;
Tin-roofed chapels
In sick towns—
O take your choice
And make your guess!

ANALOGUE

Men who care for the slow
Headswinging walk of a bull;

Whose hopes and dread rise
In the blade, bend with a stalk;
Who will explain each whim
Of angered, joking Fate
By marrying seasons and proverbs;
Their hands knotted and learned
In lifting a pick; who know
How pain and weather can baulk
All plans: such folk, when dear
Demeter's ground lay warm
And dry with almond husks
And myrtle and would owe
Remembrance to the dead,
Argued, as men today
Talk, in *The Barley Mow*,
Of ghosts and penalties.

Men whose faces are stern,
For the rungs shake under them
As they climb different ladders
To consolation, and turn
In dispute or vertigo:
'Credo,' they call like birds,
Then, 'Curro.' Aware of doctrine
And the great hazard of words,
Their skin creeping, their nerves
Taut in effort to learn
For certain the logic of grace:

Beside a gas-fire, in cloister,
Study or abbey—shut off
By intellect from the day,
Not heeding if last night's rain
Harmed or was southerly kind
To the breeding earth—their concern
Is souls and punishment.

HISTORY

Was it an age
Brilliant and languishing,
As when the air's soft
And almost cloudy,
While colossal raindrops
Hang in the hedge?
Or was it an age
Of summer tiredness,
When people quarrelled
As they rested on benches,
And along gravel paths
Of the gardens, children
Played and cried?

ROSS ABBEY

The cowpat track and dusty bramble leads
To childhood's riverwet and glistening meads.
O dear Ross Abbey! ruined, with a tree
Grown through you, how your presence lived in me
With images, persistent and devout,
Of brother, weed and water, frog and trout,
Until that middle-aged, that rainy day
I saw you once again, then looked away.

Sadder to meet some face where power once shone
And find its whole authority now gone . . .

FUNERALS

Be done with show. Let the dead go to their lair
Unseen, a light step barely heard on the stair.

ORIGINS

1

Thinness of music far away—
Repeated thuds, a few high notes,
Are all one hears—how well this teases
Memory, angers the brain.
Towards me in the same way floats
A sense of forbears long ago
Distressing as that distant playing:
For it can never be made clear,
What did our predecessors fear?
How did they talk? When did they smile?
Were they uneasy in their souls?

2

A wind blows along the quays.
Rigging slats. Hawsers creak.
Here they stumble: in big hands
Smaller hands that pinch and tweak;
Coming from the barest mountain
Or a quiet of flat lands
To cities smoking in the dusk,
To pestilence and grime that's both
On water and the merchant-desk:
Those ancestors, those falling leaves
That as they rot make green my growth.

3

Before them—pedlar, diplomat,
Landlord, peasant—these speak low,
Whistle, curse, stamp their feet;
That one greasy as his hat,
This one laughing from conceit.
All mine. As for the women: some
Have a scent of melancholy sedge,
Or laurels in wet woods; others
Rock slowly on high balconies
Under a charring sun; and some
Are rags along a gutter's edge.

4

Could my variable power
Of thought derive from difference
Of fancies they were racked with—could
It stem from their belief in arches
Made of angels' wings, from fret
Of learning, or from schemes sad
As rain that falls from winter larches?
And some ghastly call of wit
Come from where there was a joke
Before a murder—now where flit
Jackdaws in the ivied tower?

5

Back further yet, guessing the way,
To find out from what line I'm bred:
To black tents of a restless brood,
Curdled sky, unending plains,
Horses stamping in a cold
Hard as were the Nails folk say
The gipsies forged. Or still more old
And doubtful: to a vanished mark
Of some forgotten town whose men,
In rustle of silvered silks, unshadowed
Night during a faint dog's bark.

6

Beyond such silting up, such tracts
Of time, appear the paradisal
Leaves: this moist and sheltering sight
Of the great garden, dense, entire
With fruit all year, and flying lizards
Settling in the tree of life,
Wings folded; and the sweet thorn-apple
Sharpening minds into a knife—
This land which none need go from, past
The distant, guardian sword of fire
That wavers to the left and right.

7

However vast and ancient are these
Epochs, all of them seem mirrored
In my temper, which can feel
Walled in, or else defenceless, eager
And thrusting like armies, soft as sand,
Cast down like cities; never still
But moving on to a new land
Or climate, all in a few hours—
Contracted but exact, as after
Rain the storm-filled sky lours
In the smallest rut. But if

8

There was an age yet earlier,
North of the dank Caucasian pass,
Before the everburning fields
And Tartarus the triple-moated
Town, and near the iron-throated
Mountain coughing brass and steel—
Then, as a woman, I have found
What we inherit in our blood
From those bereaved by the first wastes
And wailing for their menfolk drowned
In utter darkness of the flood.

THE DOG

Calm in their age, these city walls
Stand with full dignity at night,
Consoling men for what appals
And horrifies the woken sight.

Far down, low in the ditch, by stones
This urban power is founded on,
Some dog, sniffing for scraps or bones,
Feeling a sudden apprehension,

Yelps. And gathers answering yelp
And bark to reassure it. Oh
My soul, what can I do to help
Your guilt that lurks and runs below?

WHILE SATYRS HUNTED FOR A NYMPH

While satyrs hunted for a nymph
As we for strawberries in a wood,
Philosophers, their blood and lymph
Excited by the search for Good,

Found Cause in Space; and tracked Despair
In Time; felt human Destiny
And Reason swaying in the air
Like a bee-tumbled peony;

Perceived (but never told their School)
Truth transparent as a shrimp
Darting backwards in a pool;
And Thought with all its tendons limp.

They are gone. Their counter-pleas
Of proof have left us, every one,
Like sailors thirsting for a breeze—
And still the breeze drops with the sun.

A CONJURATION

Away, all anguish harrowing the mind
   And ruffling harbours of mankind
With fears. Be off! Leave me alone to quell
   Such dread by fernseed, cloak or spell.
Pretending, then, to conjure up one hour
   Of whole and unmolested power,
I call for noon prolonged. And let it be
   The summer of my days; agree
That flowering lindens or the fig should grow,
   And shade of currants, where I go;
Let seeding grasses touch my legs and nudge
   Their plumes, that Rhadamanthus, judge
And ruler in Elysian fields, might bless
   Such clear and easy happiness.
With no attainment here, and no degree
   Of failure, rid of humours, free

From hoping for the whisper of a name
  Along dark rushing halls of Fame,
I find delusion and her sighs in flight;
  And gently as the sea at night
Breathes on a southern shore, the senses fall
  Assenting and forgiven. All
Who travel home on hay-floats, warm and tired,
  Will know my thoughts: this calm desired
And won, this moment when Oceanus flows
  Round into itself, this doze
That gains full strength to find and climb the steep
  Smooth orchard ladder into sleep.

SECTIO DIVINA

        The heart sings
Of Colchis in whose forests once wild aurochs hid
        Till Jason ploughed with them—
        O happy farmer Jason;
        As it sings of the splashed hem
        Of barefoot women on
A shore, stooping, looking in the rocks for squid
        While the sea rages to condemn
        All tamed and gentle things.

        Because of savagery preferred,
        Soft the lost cause, the trusting bird:

Cahow and parrot with their cry
Gone from Bermuda; in our eye
The image lies reversed, and slaughter
Fearfully must burn the water.

Cures are found
In plants, or else where beaches lie most derelict.
Gaze, soul, at the spiral
Of a shell; count,
In a fircone's wooden coronal,
How gnomons can surmount
Opposing forces with the mediating, strict
And Golden Mean, whose wiles are all
Displayed in tide and ground.

EVEN SO

In spite of striding
Lean-legged John's
Flame of words
In the wilderness;

And orators
Who stand in bronze,
Braving both
The rain and birds—

None the less,
Just as dogs
Must always lap
At filthy puddles,

So the fishwives'
Hands will chap,
Roofs fall loose
And walls get sick.

In spite of garlic
Breath of Rome
And senators;
In spite of lives

Good as fables;
Envoys, tired
And fidgeting
At treaty tables—

Children still
Have pecked-out lungs;
The old maid slanders
All around;

Hope, like a fox,
Has gone to ground;
And crowds feel hate
That burns their tongues.

127

POISONED IN SEARCH OF THE
MEDICINE OF IMMORTALITY

When Hsüang Tsung, great emperor,
Giddy and ill, carried in a litter,
Saw the stars sway,

His conquests and his arguments
And powers, falling into fever with him,
Pulsed their lives away.

Bow to his shade.   To be at rest
Is but a dog that sighs and settles: better
The unrelenting day.

EPIPHANY IN A COUNTRY CHURCH

Rough-fisted winter and the blurred organ join
In minds of villagers to bring
A smell of wheatstraw under hoofs and sanfoin
In hay where beasts are fattening.

What does it matter if our wise men stress
The Barn as false, the Feast as wrong?
I hold the Magi were the wiser, yes,
To be believed in for so long.

A January mist how hides the wood;
Hard facts are overlaid by myth:
In us these last keep company, and should,
Like heart and bones in Farmer Smith,

Who kneels to pray. Rubbing his neck—If beef
Goes up this month, he thinks . . . Round him
Confer vague consolations, powers of grief,
Man's fear and the high cherubim.

WAR AND PEACE

'Lately I cried with men.
Now once again
I wait for the slack of the tide,
Watch for a smooth in the wave and drop
My lobsterpots
Down between the grey rocks:
In the wet rope
Strong hope.

'The violence I was in,
Its crash and din
Are gone. My dear one, nothing breaks
When she holds it or tumbles from her lap
Save when she starts up

Quickly to greet me or give me to sup:
In the folds of her dress
Gentleness.'

ON LOOKING DOWN A STREET

My mind's disturbed as rooks in the air . . .
May a thin-shouldered mountain hare
Or shy and meditative donkey,
Cat that gallops down an alley
And the squint-eyed, sandy dab,
Curlew, spider, vole and crab—
Creatures both severe and great
Or nimble as hens running under a gate—
Pray for me now. Lord, how I need
Their cleverness, their careful speed
Or power to be still, their sense,
Their pride and total innocence!
To keep from being fool or wretch
Till the hearse-horses trot this stretch.

Poems, 1949–1954

EVERYMAN IN THE WILDERNESS

'Our own God travelled in his Ark
In step with us, by day, by dark.
The little landcrabs scuttled by
Like fears, transparent and too sly
For us to glimpse their homes. Our feet
Moved in scant grass; then manna, sweet
And trembling on the branch, was left
For boulders, shale and scree and cleft
Which, gasping, we yet had to climb . . .'
Such was their song. O cheating Time!
You will not, while the world unrolls
A curious design for souls,
Help those who have been glancing back
On old Egyptian wrongs and the black
Bruise of guilt for even longer
Than the Jews: you still defer
That green peace and the crops and sheep
Men see ahead and crave to keep.

Children now awake to birds.
Mortals rose to words
Fresh as the morning

When clover and the far hawks,
Scabious and meadow-larks
Shadowed a searing

That ran along nerve and sense,
To mend a bad conscience
By caustic of loving.

Tax-collector and prostitute:
Perhaps they were astute,
More understanding

Than open throats, festered teeth,
Slovenly wits and breath
Gaping and crowding,

Or than any tolling-tongued
Masters who had wronged
Life with their learning.

Gently or fiercely, to all around
    He would explain, expound,
        Like a dog leaping

Through tall stalks of wheat:
    Such was the pounce and feat
        Of this debating;

Till an attic room rang
    With a sad air sung
        After the supping.

Destiny and darkness flow
    Faster, now, than low
        Clouds that are falling;

His friend snores, head to rock;
    The world takes stock,
        Hardly breathing.

Thinking how steepled jealousy,
    Prim-lipped authority,
        Pride of condemning

Can derive from that despair,
    Sleep, lantern, unfair
        Act of denying,

Warmth drains out of us. The soul
  Shown in its goodness, whole:
    No hammering

Of flesh to wood can harm that proof.
  Yet man is without roof
    And night is freezing.

A TUSCAN FARMER

Why praise the huge past works of Hercules
When he leans idly on his club in Rome?
Come to my farm instead; walk round my home
When autumn puts its ladder in the trees
And what was stripped two thousand years ago
Is stripped again, or ploughed, made into stacks
And ricks and bundled heaps, by arms and backs
Aching with thrift. The least of plants that grow
As fodder have to fight the drought: my oxen,
Going softly, pull with as great a strain.
Each clod, and hanging leaf, and wild grass cane
Is stronger than that strongest of all men
Whose lion, hydra, hell-dog, mares and boar
Were overcome indeed, but once, no more.

JANUS

1

A draught blown
Through January's door
Touches hard eyelids, chilled by night,
Of Two-Face, overseer
And guardian, who has always known
That warm and secret rite
Behind him, and the clear
Sharp light
Of any coming year.
Along this street, poor
Shutters, all thrown
Crookedly together, have their hinges closed
On shames, joys,
Longing and dread,
Restless and exposed
In dreams whose poise
Tilts back then leans ahead—
As if souls could explore
And fly in shuttlecock and battledore
Between life and the dead—
Till the town grumbles, clatters, gains its sight
And the last sleeper shakes,
Opens his mouth, wakes
And, jumping out of bed,
Uncombs the tangled morning noise.

And what if ships
Should break the distant skin of the sea?
Or plague or worm provide
Disaster for each olive-tree?
That is a last years' story—
As today our lips
Forget rope, wind and tide,
Reasons and orders, while they speak
Of what we see:
A drop of water
Trembling in its slide
Along a sparrow's beak;
The blowsy girl who'll tweak
And laugh, pulling a little daughter
By her dress
Back to the old one's hips
Sunk down in massive happiness;
Or of a child who runs
With gutter treasure
To his mother while her face is like the sun's
Full pleasure
As her arms and knees
Jiggle the baby: fondness
Has no measure:
Newness no comparisons.

VENICE PRESERVED

Under the mingled bongle booming
Of St. Mark's, the pigeon-whirring,
Death black shade and seablown hopes,
Light has to dance and ripple. Copes
Of gold speak to the sun out loud
And crocus-mitres pierce a crowd
Where pistolled guards, and choirboys, state
In shy and swaying, shuffling gait,
A ceremony old as dreams.
O fond Evangelist: here gleams
His silvered, sleeping effigy
To dazzle hearts; then, dry and grey,
Skull and legbones under glass
Joggle at shoulder level, pass
Old men and Mickey Mouse balloons
While jews'-harps buzz and plainchant swoons
And postcard sellers, touts and pimps
Keep up their trade. A woman limps,
Pulls her shawl tighter, with a tear
Sees the slow walkers disappear,
And puts thick fingers on her mouth
To kiss the whole warm, saintly South.

To lipping sounds of water, dark
As dissolution, we embark
Among these stones that weep in grandeur

For such hovels; for the slur
Of palaces whose bricks are cracked
From old decay or greed and racked
By ills; and for a poverty
That dreads a winter. Now, most gently,
Are we shivering in moonlight
As if lovesick, while the night
Reveals each column, balustrade,
Dome and doorway,—unafraid
Of placards for some brand of gin
Where steamer-wash comes nosing in,
Or trash, or shabby songs : all merge,
Uplifted like a bridge's surge.
In her unbroken dignity
This trollop crumbles; painted, easy,
Filled with power to exploit
Prodigious charms and still adroit
In voice and beauty, she cajoles
Fine, votive answers from our souls.

CALENDAR

1

Too clean, the infant year, too new
And snowy innocent: it hides from view
Old rooted grudge and sin.

2

But memory floods to an edge
Of dark and bitter February sedge
That shivers like our skin,

3

And doubts are colder than the hands
Of men who harrow the long pasturelands
In painful discipline:

4

Until high mercy will assuage
The heart, and show it April's missal-page
Alive upon the ground.

5

Lovers now welcome thunderskies:
Their shock, the shelter, and a flash of eyes
That can be strange, profound,

6

Then tender as the fledgling days
Of June, when beauty trembles in the haze
With every rustling sound.

7

The halfway month. A pause for fears
Of middle-age, a deskful of arrears,
Time sped, so little done,

8

As heat lies heavy on the land.
Dogs snap at flies. Few tempers can withstand
The slowness of the sun,

9

Those parks that shrivel, leaves that spoil,
The sad allotments dug in a sour soil
Where towns and grime have won:

10

We need to feel gross sacks of grain
And in them, deities of earth and rain,
To put our sickness right.

11

The cake has crumbled, fires are lit.
Pink-pawed and back humped up, a mouse will sit
And nibble in quick fright,

12

And old, fat-fingered oaks are bare
While stars wheel through the empty, frozen air
To the slow hum of night.

A CLERICAL SQUIRE

Warm by the fire,
Toe in slipper,
Swinging his foot:
A clerical squire.
Where did he pass?
Outside, the Dipper
Ignores the spire.
Cold as brass,
Sour as soot,
Are death and desire.

THE HUNTER

Now show me any whole truth
Sustained as summer was in youth,
Plain and bare as winter trees,
Glittering like Ligurian seas,
Found in haycocks and in spires
Or lapping under hawser wires,
Burnt by meteor, scratched by fowl,
Alive in nudge and grin and scowl,
Proud as rags that sit alone,
Stronger than a dolmen stone,
As impertinent and wild
As a rough-haired tinker's child,

Sudden, like a gannet's dive,
Yet close and warm as honey-hive.

Because an old, obsidian face
Looks down in disillusioned grace;
Because, with pebbles spurting fear,
Siddhartha and his charioteer,
Fleeing through moonlight, found decay
And death and suffering on their way;
Because a half-wheel pulls a bell
And half a truth will serve to tell
Bewildered people; and a flash
Of dazzling knowledge gave one gash
To time when the great Doctor saw
His tomes, his tomes summed up as straw:
Shall I not ransack, search and tear
The clouds and grasses with my snare?

Notes

NOTES

Quotation on title-page. This is from Quarles's *Emblems*, where it is attributed to Hugo, *Liber de Anima*. The following is an extract from a letter from Fr. A. Gwynn, S.J., of Dublin:

'. . . I have found the very words which Quarles quotes in a treatise *De Interiori Domo*, printed in Migne as a work wrongly attributed to St. Bernard (P.L. 184, col. 543). This treatise is sometimes given as part of *Liber de Anima*, attributed to Hugh of St. Victor. It was probably written by a Cistercian monk of the early twelfth century.

'Here are the words (*loc. cit.*):

' *De Interiori Domo*, cap. 72: *O custos cordis, quam modicum et cupidum cor habes! Parvum est et magna cupit. Vix ad unius milvi refectionem sufficere posset, et totus mundus ei non sufficit.*'

Page 35. 'youths To whom a rose', etc. The sea-battle of Lepanto in 1571 when the Turks were prevented from overrunning all Europe.

p. 35. The Chinese Reds' Long March began in October 1934 in Kiangsi (west of Shanghai) with 100,000 men and ended 368 days later in Shensi (west of Peking) with 50,000 men. They had covered 6,000 miles.

p. 40. Ronda bridge. An incident in the Spanish civil war.

pp. 41 and 42. Aldgate and the Minories. A soldier in Allenby's campaign is speaking.

p. 45. Brian Boru, King of Munster, was killed in the eleventh century. It may be remembered that at this time the Irish were chiefly engaged in fighting the Danes who had occupied Dublin.

p. 46. The court cards in some continental packs represent Rachel, Lancelot, Charles, Judith, Pallas, Lahire, Hogier, Hector, Alexandre, Caesar, David and Asine.

147

p. 57–8. These Pegasi are the heraldic supporters of a family's coat-of-arms; their bronze models guard this garden's ornamental lake.

p. 59. The dome of St. Paul's Cathedral houses a library, in a room carved by Grinling Gibbons, where for a few pence one may see one of the finest collections of lay books including this first edition of Chaucer, detailed account-books of the rebuilding of St. Paul's, subscription lists after the Great Fire and many treasures of great interest to bibliophiles. Next door, in the Muniment Room, are the documents and Royal Seals of the early English Kings, many of whom were crowned in old St. Paul's before the Norman Conquest.

The Cathedral used to be the centre of social life for the community and Londoners referred to it as 'our Paul's'. Wren designed the steps leading up to the present building to prevent the entry of donkeys loaded with merchandise; but wishing to perpetuate the best of the old tradition he originally planned his Cathedral with small rooms instead of side-chapels, where City Guilds could meet.

p. 64. 'By saint', etc. The island of Ensay in the Outer Hebrides is roughly two miles long and half a mile across, but has a very small ruin which is known as St. Columba's Cathedral.

p. 64. St. Kevin's hermit cell at Glendalough, a famous tourist sight in Co. Wicklow.

p. 65. Fortifications dug up at Megiddo revealed the Biblical 'Armageddon'.

p. 75. Erzulie. Voodoo goddess of love in Haitian rites.

p. 79. 'Pourrvou', etc. Favourite remark of Buonaparte's mother when neighbours informed her of her son's victories.

p. 80. Excavations at Thermopylæ show the truth of Herodotus' statement that the Persian host was so vast that its arrows obscured the sun. The wall of Phocias was found and repairs in it mentioned by Herodotus, also the stone posts of gates from which the name Thermopylæ was derived. No arrowheads here (from where the Spartans charged the Persians, and Leonidas was killed) but a huge mass of them was found in the hill to which his three hundred withdrew.

p. 81. A country legend, in a certain part of France, of Eve and the Garden of Eden.

p. 87. Terracotta figures from a tomb in Myrina, of turbaned and dancing winged Erotes, now in the Boston Museum of Fine Arts.

p. 109. Biblical scholarship now recognizes the likelihood of four Johns:

(1) John the Baptist;

(2) John the Apostle (son of Zebedee and brother of James) who was probably martyred with his brother in A.D. 44;

(3) John the Evangelist (John of Ephesus) who probably lived at the end of the first century and is thought to have belonged to a Sadducean, high priestly family. The last chapter of the Gospel is generally agreed to be an editorial addition. Internal evidence shows the impossibility of the Fourth Gospel's author being John the Apostle, living to a ripe old age at Ephesus.

Work of: '*Un juif hellénisant, inspiré de Philon d'Alexandrie, qui connait les Synoptiques, mais n'en fait point cas. C'est un théologien mystique, non un historien.*' S. Reinach.

'*Les récits de Jean ne sont pas de l'histoire mais une contemplation de l'Evangile; ses discours sont des méditations théologiques sur le mystère du salut.*' Prof. Loisy.

(4) St. John the Divine (John of Patmos). Book of Revelation probably written towards end of first century.

'He expressed his thoughts and feelings in barbarous Greek, disfigured by Semitic use. His style is conclusive against his having been the John who wrote the Fourth Gospel.' Dr. Barnes.

p. 113. Green Mountain. The Senussi grazing lands, an escarpment at Barce, east of Benghazi and about 200 by 40 miles in size.

p. 115. Clonmacnois. Monastic settlement on the banks of the river Shannon, founded in the sixth century and now a collection of ruins.

p. 121–2. stanzas 6, 7 and 8. The following suggestions are taken from Fessenden's *The Deluged Civilization of the Caucasian Isthmus*, whose speculations on the N. Caucasian origin of man have had the support—though for different reasons—of Breasted and Flinders Petrie:

Caspian, Balkasch and Aral Sea are remains, not dried up, of a far larger sea which was once connected with the Arctic Ocean and also, via Manytsch lakes, with Sea of Azov and Black Sea.

When this larger sea was in being, the earliest civilization was possibly established in N. Caucasus.

Mankind would have had no incentive to leave this locality bounded northward by ice, to the west by a vast morass infested by mosquitoes (Herodotus' 'bees'), to the east by the Everburning Fields (Baku oilfields) and the sea, and to the south by the seemingly impassable range of the Caucasus; also rich in fire (spontaneously ignitable naphtha), metal ores, timber, alluvial soil, irrigating streams, useful animals, fruit, grain. Mountain of Iron and Brass nearby (Mt. Thammuzeria or Tamischieria).

With the melting of the ice-cap, the enlarged Caspian (mentioned above) flooded westward and forced discovery of Pass of Dariel (or Erebus) near Mt. Kasbek through the Caucasus and into a region known in Semitic times as Aidon, or more exactly East Aidon.

Erebus, a 500 ft. deep cleft, runs due north and south in lat. 43° so that its forbidding defile is dark even in summer. Its fortified gates (Iron Gates) said to have been placed there by K. Aidoneus (king of Aidon).

Beyond the pass, western and middle portion of valley was called Aidon by Semites, also called Aethiopia by Phoenicians, and later, Colchis by the Greeks. The middle portion, East Aidon —walled in by mountains on all four sides and into which the Gate opened—is the *Paradeisos*, or enclosed park, of the Septuagint, and Garden of Eden of Semites. Eastern third of valley, through which R. Alizon flows, called *Elysion* by Greeks.

Vegetation of Garden of Eden luxuriant and dense, with fruit-trees bearing wild fruit, all year round flowers and thick pasturage. Genesis, and Strabo (whose great-uncle was Governor of Colchis) both state very heavy dew watered portion where little rain fell, so never any drought.

Tree of Life; Golden Apples of the Hesperides. Greek tradition says fruit coloured gold and like an apple, prolonging life but guarded by a dragon. Ezekiel says tree guarded by cherubim (Kirubi) with four feet and four wings, like dragons. Creatures which would answer this description are now found in Malaya, in the form of flying lizards: Amagidae, or *draco volans*. They are brightly coloured, look like a snake when their wings are folded, and are partial to *Citrus medica*. 'Upon thy belly thou shalt go' has meaning when applied to these beautiful flying reptiles. *Citrus medica* has remarkable healing properties for wounds; helps the intestinal tract; has a high vitamin content.

Tree of Knowledge of Good and Evil: the thorn-apple (*Datura-matel*) acts like a drug to induce great mental acuity, followed by depression; highly appetizing; an aphrodisiac; can also give violent delirium. Fumes of it when burnt have same effect.

'He placed at the east of the Garden of Eden the Kirubi, and the flame of a sword which turneth every way.' Sword probably a fired oilwell in what is now the Baku district, visible for great distances.

p. 126. Cahow. A seabird of Bermuda, extinct since the seventeenth century. It had an extraordinary cry (giving the Island a reputation for being filled with strange sounds and supernatural beings—'The Tempest') and was so tame and easy to catch, as well as good to eat, that it was soon exterminated by the early settlers.

p. 126. Gnomon. Any figure which can be added to, so that the resultant whole still retains the original shape.

To make a gnomonic rectangle, take a figure whose sides are in the proportion of 1 to ·618. Add a square to the longer side. The whole new rectangle will be the same shape as the first. Add a square to the longer side of the new figure, and so on. . . .

The spiral which can be traced from the boundaries of such figures is the spiral of the whelk and nautilus, turban shell and snail. Not only do most shells grow in this gnomonic fashion, but the most common arrangements of leaves round a stem, petals in flowers, and scales in a fir-cone, follow the ratio of:

$$0 : 1, 1 : 2, 3 : 5, 8 : 13, 21 : 34, 55 : 89, 144 : \text{etc.}$$

(See Sir D'Arcy Thompson's *On Growth and Form*.)

This is the series of what are sometimes called the Fibonacci numbers, which can be written as:

$$\frac{0}{1}, \frac{1}{2}, \frac{3}{5}, \frac{8}{13}, \frac{21}{34}, \text{ etc.}$$

If these fractions are worked out, they are seen to get nearer and nearer to 0·618, in other words, to converge to the number mentioned earlier. This number (0·618) was well known to the ancients, who called it the *sectio divina* or Golden Mean.

The mechanical stresses of growth call for a special solution, if the thing that grows is to keep its orderly and original shape; and it is curious and lovely to see with what frequency and elegance Nature provides the gnomon as the answer to anarchy.